RESOURCE BANK
Book 3

Dedication
To Rebekah and Rachael, Tom and Grace
and
Laurie with thanks

RESOURCE BANK
Book 3

by Margaret Cooling and Diane Walker
with Maggie Goodwin

British and Foreign Bible Society
Stonehill Green, Westlea, SWINDON SN5 7DG, England

A catalogue record for this book is available from the British Library
ISBN 0 564 08575 8

Printed in Great Britain by Stanley L. Hunt (Printers) Ltd.

Cover design and illustrations by Jane Taylor

Bible Societies exist to provide resources for Bible distribution and use. The British and Foreign Bible Society (BFBS) is a member of the United Bible Societies, an international partnership working in over 180 countries. Their common aim is to reach all people with the Bible, or some part of it, in a language they can understand and at a price they can afford. Parts of the Bible have now been translated into over 1,900 languages. Bible Societies aim to help every church at every point where it uses the Bible. You are invited to share in this work by your prayers and gifts. Bible Society in your country will be very happy to provide details of its activity.

CONTENTS

ACKNOWLEDGEMENTS

The authors gratefully acknowledge the help of Linda Armitt, Ruth Cooper, Karen Edgington and Mabel Lie in the preparation of this manuscript. Our thanks also go to Jean Mead for contributing the activity in Book 2, page 27, to Sue Hatherly for advice and ideas for music activities, to Gillian Crow for checking certain factual details and to Trevor Cooling for writing the Introduction. The activity on page 101 was developed from an activity which appeared in *Assemblies for the Summer Term* (RMEP).

We would also like to thank Dr John Goldingay, Dr Stephen Travis, both of St John's Theological College, Nottingham, Sid Freeman and Helen Thacker for reading and commenting on different parts of the manuscript. Final responsibility for any errors of course lies with the authors alone.

We also wish to thank Elaine Walker and the pupils and staff of the following schools for testing material:

Albany Junior School, Stapleford • Bramcote Church of England (Aided) Primary School, Nottingham • Bramcote Hills Primary School, Nottingham Brambletye Middle School, Surrey • The Manor Primary School, Romford Stevenson Junior School, Stapleford • St. John's Church of England (Controlled) Primary School, Stapleford • St Paul's Church of England (Aided) Primary School, Hereford • Stoneleigh First School, Ewell • William Lilley Infant School, Stapleford

This book has been produced under the auspices of the Stapleford Project.

The Stapleford Project is a curriculum development initiative based at Stapleford House Education Centre. The project aims to produce materials and offer in–service training to support the teaching of Christianity in schools.

Stapleford House Education Centre is the national conference and study centre of the Association of Christian Teachers. Full details of courses and of publications sponsored by the centre are available from: Stapleford House Education Centre, Wesley Place, Stapleford, Nottingham, NG9 8DP

INTRODUCTION

The place of the Bible in primary school religious education

For as long as there has been formal schooling the Bible has found a place in the classroom. However, its effective use in school religious education is an issue which continues to generate controversy, sometimes quite heated.

The history of the use of the Bible

A brief study of the syllabuses appearing after the 1944 Education Act makes it immediately apparent that religious education and teaching the Bible were considered synonymous at the time. The content of the Bible was the one thing that the different Christian denominations who were involved in drawing up these syllabuses could agree on.

However, in the mid–1960s Ronald Goldman published two highly influential studies on children's understanding of the Bible, which seriously undermined teachers' confidence in these syllabuses. His results seemed to show that the Bible was, to put it simply, too difficult for young children to understand. He claimed that it was not a children's book and that they would develop serious misunderstandings if introduced to its complex theological ideas at too young an age.

Confidence in the Bible as a suitable book for primary schools was further damaged by the rejection of the so–called "confessional" approach to religious education with which it was associated. This was based on the assumption of the truth of Christianity and had as its goal the transmission of the Christian faith to children. It was discredited because it was seen as indoctrinatory in that it both ignored other religions and did not allow children the freedom to choose their beliefs for themselves.

The multifaith approach to religious education, which replaced the confessional approach, has, however, also been a major factor in re–establishing confidence in the Bible as an "educational" book in recent years. In this approach it is recognized that sacred texts are central to religion, and educational justice cannot be done if children are not introduced to them. The Bible has been rediscovered as the living book of the Christians, alongside the Qur'an in Islam, the Guru Granth Sahib in Sikhism and so on. This regaining of confidence has been further enhanced by the realization that Goldman's theories do not take enough account of the way in which children learn religious ideas. It is now widely felt that there were some serious shortcomings in his work.

The current use of the Bible in primary schools

Although in theory the Bible has a valid place in modern religious education, the evidence is that it is not used particularly well. The research carried out by Dr Leslie Francis in primary schools in Gloucestershire,[1] and various reports by Her Majesty's Inspectors of Schools indicate that:

(i) Bible stories are often selected at random with little attention being given to their religious message. A widely quoted example of this is where the story of Jesus feeding 5,000 people is used as part of a piece of work designed to persuade children not to drop litter.

(ii) Little guidance is given in schemes of work on criteria for selection of stories, the important religious ideas to be explored or the level at which stories should be approached.

(iii) The range of biblical material taught is so narrow that the same stories are used over and over again and are often presented in an educationally undemanding fashion.

(iv) Little attention is given to the biblical context and background of the stories used.

Ian Birnie captures the situation well when he describes current use as reducing "the Bible to a history book, a book of moral stories and fables or worse still to a source of proof texts for what is claimed to be the Christian faith and life."[2] The ideal that children should appreciate it as the living book of the Christians is rarely attained.

Controversies surrounding the use of the Bible in schools

Although many teachers are including biblical material in their teaching, many also express anxiety about whether they are doing the right thing for their children. There are four particular issues which underlie this anxiety:

1. The Bible is not a child's book

It is here that the continuing influence of Goldman's work is strongest. Basically the fear is that by introducing children to biblical material too early they will develop crude ideas in the order of "God is an old man in the sky". Like the Russian cosmonaut who announced to the world that he had been "there" and not found God, they will reject these when they begin to mature in their thinking. Two things can be said about this.

Firstly, it is a fact that learning in all subjects proceeds by children refining their understanding of concepts. For example, many children have a scientifically crude idea of an atom as a collection of solid balls. However, they do not reject the concept of the atom *per se* as they learn more and realize the mistaken nature of their childhood ideas. Rather, under the guidance of good teaching, they become more refined in their thinking. Likewise, with religion children have many crude ideas. It is true that these are "mistaken" when compared with sophisticated theological thinking, but they are not "mistaken" if by that it is meant that children should never hold such ideas. Indeed it seems likely that such childhood "mistakes" are essential if children are going to be able to develop more sophisticated modes of thought in the future. The role of the teacher is to help children build on their "mistakes" by providing new experiences and opportunities for conversation which encourage them to refine their thinking. We should not underestimate a child's capacity to do this.

Secondly, it is becoming increasingly clear that one of the reasons why children have difficulty in handling biblical material is because it so often makes no sense to them in their own world of experience. Religious ideas have to be related to, or earthed in, children's experience if they are going to be successfully integrated into their patterns of thinking. Otherwise they will be like a proverbial cuckoo chick in amongst their other ideas. As one writer has said about the biblical concept of salvation:

> Pupils are not going to be able to understand salvation until they have learnt what it is to be saved, not in a religious way but in all kinds of other ways — to be saved from drowning by a lifeboat, to save each week and put it in the bank, and to feel safe and tucked up for the night.[3]

In order to assist in this earthing of biblical concepts, we have included ideas for a range of activities that can be used for introducing biblical material into the classroom and have suggested links that can be made with other areas of the curriculum. Part of this process of earthing is also to encourage children to explore and develop their ability to use religious language.[4]

2. The question of miracles

Some people argue that miracle stories are inappropriate for young children. There is clearly a problem if children are encouraged to believe that biblical characters are magicians or that God's action can be invoked as a simple solution to all life's problems. However, the Bible does not treat miracles in this way, but rather places them in a context which conveys a theological message and which thereby gives a broader meaning to the event. For example the relationship of faith is a crucial element of many New Testament miracles. They are not presented as "happenings" for their own sake.

We have included a number of miracle stories in this collection because we believe it would be quite wrong to ignore them. They are part of the biblical world and many modern Christians believe that they actually took place. To exclude them would be to distort the Bible and is not something that is done with the sacred scriptures of other religions when they are used in religious education. It is, however, important that when teaching these stories they are dealt with in the context of a theme which they communicate and are also related to other biblical material which illustrates that theme. Furthermore, as with the miracle stories of other religious traditions, it is important that they are treated as the heritage of particular communities. In the classroom, study of them should be introduced by phrases such as "we are going to listen to a story which is important for Christians", which leave children free either to identify with them or not. If asked whether these stories actually happened, the best answer a teacher can give at this level is that some people believe that they did and others (including some Christians) that they did not.

3. The question of truth

This leads us to consider perhaps one of the most debated issues amongst Christian theologians, whether or not Christian faith depends on the historical accuracy of the Bible. Opinions vary across a spectrum from those who insist that it is literally true at all points, to those who regard questions of historical truth as totally irrelevant to genuine faith. The fact that scholars disagree on this issue means that it is quite wrong for teachers to assume any one position as normative. The problem is that the primary school classroom is clearly not the place for detailed and technical theological discussions. The challenge (and it is a very difficult challenge) is to remain fair to this difference of opinion without making the Bible unusable in the primary school context.

Probably the one thing that most Christians can agree on is that the Bible is not simply a description of a series of events, but is fundamentally a book with a message. In this book we have therefore concentrated on that message. To this end, we have generally taken the text at face value and have not entered into discussions of historicity. This is consistent with the way in which sacred texts from other religions are usually handled in schools. However, it may well be that children ask questions about historical truth. If so it will be important to make them aware both that there is a difference of opinion amongst Christians on this matter and that religious language employs different genres to convey a message, e.g. poetry, symbol, history, metaphor and myth. Analysis of which genre particular texts represent is not, however, the prime purpose of this book.

Some of the stories we use are particularly controversial in this respect, for example Ruth, Jonah, the siege of Jericho and the nature miracles in the New Testament. Here again we have not entered into the archaeological and textual evidence for and against their historicity. In our opinion the amount of information that is needed to make a fair and reasoned judgement is quite substantial and, furthermore, is often difficult to interpret. It simply was not possible to do justice to this in the space available. It also seemed wrong that we should present our conclusions on these debates, with the implication that there are simple answers.

Even putting aside the question of historicity, it is, of course, also true that theologians vigorously debate the question of how biblical texts should be interpreted. Inevitably, therefore, some people will disagree with our description of the message conveyed by certain passages. Again it is unrealistic for teachers in primary schools to introduce pupils to the technicalities of this theological controversy. We have therefore sought to utilize what might be called traditional interpretations, which are widely accepted amongst Christians of many different denominations. Again this is in line with the way in which the sacred texts of other religions are handled in schools. It is, however, important to realize that no book on the Bible will be neutral or objective in the interpretations it adopts. Any such book will inevitably reflect a theology which the authors find convincing. This book is no exception.

4. The relationship with Judaism

A major misunderstanding is created if it is implied that the part of the Bible which Christians call the Old Testament is only a precursor to the New Testament and not also the sacred Scripture of Judaism in its own right. The problem is that there are in fact two ways of interpreting the Old Testament/Hebrew Bible, namely the Christian and the Jewish. Although there is much common ground, sometimes Christians and Jews understand the significance of the same text in different ways. It needs to be clearly understood that in this book we have treated the Old Testament material as part of the Christian Bible. We fully appreciate the sensitivity of this issue and do not want to deny that there is an authentic Jewish treatment of these texts. We do, however, want it to be absolutely clear that in this book we are dealing with the material in its role as part of the Christian Bible.

Of course Christians utilize Jewish insights in their attempt to understand the Old Testament, but it is only honest to make plain that they do this as Christians. The inclusion in this book of practices and ideas from certain Jewish festivals is meant to underline the immense debt of Christianity to Judaism

When it comes to the New Testament there is an important issue to be taken into account. Angela Wood, a Jew and an LEA religious education adviser, paints the problem very starkly in an article where she describes her young daughter's first encounter with the Easter story at her primary school: [5] Ester, came home distraught that "we" (the Jews) should have killed Jesus and were such a horrible people. It has to be accepted that the New Testament does focus on some negative aspects of first–century Judaism. Every religion has its negative side, but it is important that children are not left with the impression that this was the total picture of the Judaism of Jesus' day. The picture needs balancing by ensuring that they are aware that Jesus himself was a Jew, as were most of his early followers, and that there were many noble, honest and God–fearing Jews around in his time. It would be a travesty if religious education were ever unwittingly to fuel anti–semitism. The danger that it might is apparent from Ester's negative feelings about her own people.

Using the Bible in school

Another important point that has to be remembered is that the various authors of the Bible had no idea that it would be used by primary schools some 2,000 or more years later! They wrote with a very different purpose in mind, namely the teaching and edification of the religious community and the announcement of their message to the world. The Bible is proclamation designed to evoke the response of faith in its readers.[6]

This means that using it in schools takes it outside of its "normal" context. The Bible was not written by a teacher as a result of a commission from an educational publisher, nor was it designed to be a quarry of stories for illustrating teaching themes. There is therefore a delicate balance to be maintained between being true to its nature as the "faith–proclaiming", sacred text of the Christian community and using it in a way that is educationally appropriate in the modern school, where belief on the part of the pupils can neither be assumed nor sought. In seeking to achieve this balance we have employed the following principles:

1. Teaching should be true to the meaning of the text
Increasingly the educational importance of teaching structural concepts rather than just passing on information, is being recognized. Thus in an influential

report on religious education it was stated that: "Concepts are the main focal point of any educational programme... concepts help us to make sense of what we observe and encounter in particular religions".[7] The key point is that the purpose of introducing biblical material is to ensure that children come to understand those concepts that are fundamental to the Christian faith and not to provide general knowledge fodder. In using the Bible in this book we have therefore tried to remain true to the underlying concepts that the text conveys. Of course scholars will, in particular cases, disagree as to what the real message is, but we have sought to utilize the consensus within mainstream Christianity. So in grouping biblical material under themes we have tried to make our selection on the basis of the meaning that is central to the text in question.

2. The use of the Bible must support the curriculum
Balanced against the requirement to represent fairly the meaning of the biblical text for Christians, is the need to use it in a way that supports the modern primary school curriculum. We have sought to achieve this in three ways:

Firstly, although we have grouped the passages according to their theological meaning we have used titles which are appropriate to the primary curriculum. For example the biblical idea of "covenant" is included under the heading of "promise", since the former would not figure in the curriculum but the latter often does.

Secondly, in selecting material for inclusion we have tried to reflect the major theological themes of the Bible. However, in certain cases a theme has been given a higher profile than it has in the biblical text, because it has traditionally been important for primary schools. For example the theme of "sharing" is present in the Bible, although it does not have the emphasis given to it in many primary schools. We have therefore included it as one that teachers will be able to utilize. Furthermore we have sometimes used a secondary idea in a particular biblical passage to illustrate the theme. For example we have used the story of the feeding of the 5,000 under the "sharing" theme, although we are very aware that the major significance of this story is the message it conveys about Jesus Christ. However, it also carries the subsidiary theme of "sharing that costs" and can therefore legitimately be used in that context, providing that its main theological theme is also pointed out.

Thirdly we have sometimes made the decision not to use particular biblical material because of the difficulty of the issues it raises. For example we have not included the biblical image of judgement as "everlasting fire" in the theme on fire. The theme of judgement is tackled elsewhere through the story of Noah, the parable of the Sheep and the Goats and under the titles of God.

Inevitably there will be those who will disagree, on either theological or educational grounds, with both our selection and grouping of the texts. We trust they will recognize the complexity of the task we have undertaken in trying to balance the need to present the Bible in a way that respects its integrity and the need to use it in a way that promotes educational goals.

3. The text should stimulate the imagination and extend thought
In rewording the biblical material we have sometimes used storytelling techniques such as flashback and reminiscence as a way of engaging the imagination. In addition there are, in places, imaginative embellishments to the

text which we trust serve to make it live for the hearers, whilst still remaining true to the central meaning. Furthermore we have, on occasions, deliberately used difficult words to provide a basis for language extension and to introduce some basic theological vocabulary.

For these reasons it is important that teachers give some introduction before using any part of this book with a class. How much is required will depend on the age and experience of the particular group involved. Background information is provided to enable teachers to set the scene as necessary. When using this the children should be told that it has been written as though a Christian were explaining to another person the significance of the passage in question for Christians.

4. The use of the Bible should respect the educational context

One thing that should be remembered is that although the Bible was originally written to persuade its readers of the truth of its message, it cannot be used in that way in most educational contexts. We therefore recommend that pupils are made aware that this is the book of the Christians, and not necessarily "their" book. It should be pointed out that the claims to truth that are made within it are those of a particular, albeit very significant, religious group. The language used in the classroom should be non–presumptive, making it clear that the pupils are learning about Christian beliefs which they are not necessarily expected to share. There should be freedom to respond in a way that is appropriate for each child. It must of course not be forgotten that one appropriate response may be belief and commitment. It is not the place of the school either to seek or to deny this. By adopting this strategy teachers will be able to remain true to the biblical intentions whilst still fulfilling their educational responsibilities.

Using the material

This book is one of three volumes which are designed to provide a quarry of accessible and easy–to–use biblical material for the busy teacher. It is a book for dipping into rather than for using systematically. Its main purpose is to provide teachers with theologically and educationally valid ways of using biblical material with children. In schools it will provide ideas for an RE–led topic, an RE component for a topic led by another subject, or for separate RE lessons or units of work. In churches it can, with appropriate adaptations, form the basis for a programme of Bible teaching with children. In the three volumes there are over one hundred Bible passages, retold to make them suitable for reading aloud, or for children to read on their own. For ease of use the passages are organized under twenty–four themes which reflect topics commonly appearing on the primary school curriculum. Each theme contains the following components:

1. Understanding the Biblical ideas

This information will give the teacher the basic theological background information needed to understand the biblical ideas which underpin the theme. The passages grouped under a theme will develop and illustrate these ideas.

2. Introducing the passages
These are various practical ideas for introducing the theme and the biblical passages to children.

3. Other useful passages
This is a list of passages which appear elsewhere in the three volumes under other theme headings, but which might also be useful in developing this particular theme.

4. Cross–curricular links
This section demonstrates how the theme can be developed through other subjects on the curriculum, indicating how the use of biblical material can form a valid part of a wider curriculum planning process. Where appropriate, links with National Curriculum subjects are indicated. The attainment targets cited are those in force at the time of writing.

Teachers will also need to refer to the syllabus of religious education used in their school to ensure that the biblical material is introduced in a way which ensures continuity and progression and fulfils statutory requirements.

5. A Christian perspective
These notes outline how each of the passages is generally interpreted by Christians. They contain information for the teacher to draw on when discussing the passages with children.

6. Points of interest
The points of interest contain background information on each of the passages which put them in context and help in understanding their meaning and significance. Again they are for teacher information and are not designed to be read out to children.

7. The passages
Under each theme heading there are four or five passages retold from the Bible which illustrate that theme. Different types of biblical material have been included, such as story, wise sayings, law and poetry, so that children can experience the different genres of literature which appear in the Bible. All the passages can be read aloud to children, although the story material is particularly suitable for use in this way. The material is designed primarily for use with junior aged children, but can be adapted to be used with other age groups.

The three volumes contain a number of extended stories, such as the Joseph saga, which are divided up into episodes. Episodes from one extended story may appear under different theme headings depending on their main emphasis. Teachers wishing to tell the whole of an extended story will find details of where the other episodes appear by referring to the "Other useful passages" section of the theme where a particular episode appears, or on the contents page of the book.

8. Photocopiable activity pages
At the end of each theme you will find a number of photocopiable pupil activity sheets. These are not meant to be used as unsupported worksheets, but are

designed as a resource for pupil work which arises out of their study of the biblical passages in that theme. Teachers are also allowed to photocopy the relevant biblical passages from this book if they wish, so that children can refer to the passage whilst using the activity sheet. On the activity sheets children are often referred to the story and asked to read it. With younger junior children it may be necessary to read the story to them.

Two final points

1. Health and safety
As in all teaching, it is essential to ensure that all materials and procedures used in the classroom are safe. For example, glues and paints should be non–toxic and kites should be flown away from power cables with gloves worn whilst holding them. All equipment should undergo regular safety checks. Please consult your school policy document and other relevant Health and Safety regulations.

2. Acts of worship
The passages are short enough to be read in an act of worship. Those grouped together under one theme could be used to create a series of "assemblies".

Activities may need to be added, including the more reflective aspects characteristic of an act of worship — for example prayers, music or a time for thinking about the theme whilst a poem is read.

Notes

1. Francis, Leslie, *Religion In The Primary School* (Collins, 1987)
2. Birnie, Ian, "Is Teaching the Bible too Dangerous a Task for Schools?" in *British Journal of Religious Education,* Vol 5:3, Summer 1983
3. Gower, Ralph, *Religious Education At The Primary Stage* (Lion, 1990)
4. Hull, John, *God–Talk with Young Children* (Christian Education Movement, 1991)
5. Wood, Angela, "Not Whether But How" in *Discernment,* Vol 6, No I, July 1992. Available from CCBI. 35–41, Lower Marsh, London, SEI 7RL
6. *See* Copley, Terence, *About The Bible* (Bible Society, 1990) for further information.
7. Westhill College, *Assessing, Recording and Reporting RE* (Westhill College, Birmingham 1991) p 23

National Curriculum Attainment Targets

Key: M=Maths E=English S=Science T=Technology A=Art MU=Music G=Geography H=History

SECTION	ACTIVITY	Page Number	M	E	S	T	A	MU	G	H
Messages from God	Graffiti Wall	9		1,2,3						
	Messengers	10		2, 3		1	1			
	Alliteration	11–12		2, 3						
	Important Messages	13		1, 2						
Special Stories of Jesus	Stories in Glass	23		1, 2						
	Miracle Plays	24		1, 2						
	The Yeast	25	1, 4	1, 2	1, 3					
	Lost and Found	26		1, 2						
Jesus 1	Temptation	36–37		1, 2						
	Jesus the Man	38–39		2		1, 2				
	Welcome	40–41		2, 3						
	I Am	42		1						
Jesus 2	Servant Master	53		1, 2						
	The Sun	54		2,		1, 2				
	The Key to the Kingdom	55–56		2, 3						
	The Cross Symbol	57		1						
Prayer	Different Prayers	68–69		2, 3						
	The Pharisee and the Tax Collector	70		2, 3						
	Arrow Prayers	71–72		2, 3						
	Candles and Incense	73–74		3						
God	Icons	84–85					1, 2			
	God's Eyes	86				1, 2				
	Celebrating God the Provider	87–88		1, 2		1, 2				
	A Multi–sided Shape	89–90	1, 4	3						

RESOURCE BANK 3: INTRODUCTION

SECTION	ACTIVITY	Page Number	M	E	S	T	A	MU	G	H
The Holy Spirit	Wool Winding	98–99		1			1			
	Symbols of the Spirit	100					1, 2			
	Reaping the Fruit Harvest	101		2, 3			1			
	Wind Words	102		3		1, 2				

SECTION	ACTIVITY	Page Number	M	E	S	T	A	MU	G	H
Standing Up for what You Believe	In the Pit	112–113		2			1			
	Roman Soldiers	114		2, 3						
	The Daniel Jazz	115		2				1, 2		
	Standing Up for your Beliefs	116		2, 3						

Understanding the biblical ideas

Christians belive in a God who communicates. The prophet Amos remarked that, "God does nothing without telling his servants the prophets." God calls Abraham from Ur, and speaks to Moses from the burning bush. He speaks to Moses "face to face" as a man speaks to his friend. He speaks directly to the child Samuel, and sends Belshazzar a message which appears as writing on the wall. To Joseph, Pharaoh, Nebuchadnezzar and many others, God speaks in special dreams or visions.

God's word to humanity came in many forms. God spoke through the prophets who delivered the message in verbal, dramatic or written form. Jeremiah got his message of future slavery across by wearing a slave yoke. The idea of "God's Word" is a very active concept. It is not just sound, not just squiggles on paper. The Word of God is seen as active and powerful. Creation was accomplished with no more than a word from God.

The messages were not always well received. Amos was told to go home. Elijah receives a death note and had to run for his life. Several attempts were made on Jeremiah's life and he was badly treated throughout his ministry. When he wrote down his message and sent it to the king, the king chopped it up and threw it in the fire.

Messages from God can have many functions. Paul lists these when he writes to Timothy. The message may reprove, correct, encourage, instruct or train. The gospel message may be received in many ways. The parable of the sower is about receiving the message.

The message in the New Testament is described as "gospel", literally good news — the good news of the coming of Jesus and of the love and forgiveness of God. It is a message Christians are told to pass on. The ultimate message is Jesus himself, a "living word". Christians believe Jesus, in his person and life, shows what God is like. He is a living message from God.

Introducing the passages

Discuss the different ways of sending messages. Read a variety of the stories suggested to see the different ways in which God communicates with people.

Moses speaks to God directly, as does Samuel. Elijah hears a small voice. God speaks to others through prayer or story. The parables can be used to illustrate this last point.

Messages can be direct or coded. Children can invent their own codes or look at recognized codes such as Morse. Sometimes the message within a parable is difficult to find. The disciples found it difficult to understand the parable of the sower. Jesus "decoded" it for them. In Jesus' case the parable was not to stop people understanding his message but to enable them to work it out for themselves. Belshazzar's message also needed "decoding". Explore the different ways in which messages are received, and read the story of "The Sower" and "Jeremiah in the Pit".

Other useful passages

The rest of the Christmas story can be found in Book 2, pages 106, 107–108.

The section called "Prayer" is about communication with God. This can be found on pages 62–67.

Jonah refuses to deliver God's message in the stories "Jonah Runs Away", Book 1, page 96, and "Jonah gets Cross", Book 1, page 82.

God speaks to Moses and Elijah in the stories of "The Burning Bush", Book 2, page 77, and "Elijah Meets God", page 80.

Jeremiah suffers because he delivers God's message in "Jeremiah in the Pit", page 108.

Jesus is seen as a living message by Christians. See the sections headed "Jesus", pages 31–52 and "Special Stories of Jesus", pages 18–22, for suitable material.

Special dreams or visions are seen as one way in which God sends messages. See the stories of

Joseph, Book 2, pages 6–7, 67–68; Daniel, Book 2, page 8; Ezekiel, page 94, and the Christmas story, Book 2, page 106. Please emphasize these are special dreams.

Angels are God's messengers. They can be seen in stories on the following pages: Book 2, pages 47, 66, 78, 91, 107; Book 3, pages 8, 51, 52.

Cross–curricular links

English
- List all the ways in which we can communicate: talking, writing, gesture, facial expression, etc. (3)
- Specifically list purposes of writing: think about audience and purpose. (3)
- Look at hidden messages — particularly the use of rebus messages. (2)
- Write a story based on a "Message in a Bottle". (3)
- Look at signs which give messages such as road signs and pub signs. What is the difference between a sign and a symbol? (3)

Music
- Send a musical message to your friend. Make up an advertising jingle — what message would you give? Listen to jingles on tape from well–known products. Can you identify the advertisement? What messages do the adverts send? (1)
- Listen to parts of *Belshazzar's Feast* by Walton. (2)

Science
- Explore hidden messages using different types of disappearing inks such as lemon juice. (1, 3)
- Investigate colour messages in the animal and plant world. (2)
- Test out the four conditions mentioned in the parable of the sower. (2)

Technology
- Use computer generated graphics to give a warning message. It could be a fire hazard or some other warning. Design you own advertisement. What do you need to stress to get your message across? (1, 2)

Mathematics
- Explore number codes and mathematical messages. (1, 2, 3)

History
- Look at the message of the Celtic mission and the Augustinian mission in the history unit "Invaders and Settlers". (1)
- Look at the way the message of Christianity was spread by Christian missionaries during the Victorian era and how it was spread in the Americas ("Explorations and Encounters"). Look at good and bad practices. Draw up a code of good practice. (1, 2, 3) (EAT 3)

Personal and Social Education
- How do people show Christ's message of "Love One Another" in their lives? List three occasions when you have been unselfish. (EAT 3)
- Look at body language: say something nice whilst using threatening body language. Give the same message in four different styles, e.g. warm and positive, cold and negative, sarcastic, etc. (EAT 1)

Geography
- Look at the use of symbols in geography and the meanings they enshrine. (1)
- Map out the route of one of Paul's journeys. Work out the distances he covered to spread the gospel. Mark on it the destinations of his letters. (1, 2)

Art
- Look at icons. What is the icon saying about the person painted? *The Orthodox Tradition* by G Crow is very helpful. This is available from the South London RE Centre, Kilmorie Road, Forest Hill, SE23 2SP. (2)
- What is Celtic art saying? The circle is a symbol of eternity, the unending lines are a sign of continuing life. (2)

SAMUEL LISTENS TO GOD
1 Samuel 2.12–26; 3 ▶ *page 5*

A Christian perspective
Christians believe in a God who communicates. He is not a distant God who never speaks. In this story he bypasses the important person (Eli) and speaks to someone of low status, a child. Christians today do not usually hear a voice as Samuel did: sometimes God speaks through a quiet voice inside, through the Bible or through other people.

God champions the ordinary people who have no one else to look after them. Evil is not allowed to go unchecked. Not only does it cause suffering, but it is also an insult to a just and loving God. Eli's sons were stealing the part of the animals people used in their sacrifice to God. Stealing from the collecting plate would be a minor version of the same thing. The irony is that Samuel later had two sons who did not follow their father's good example, just as Eli's sons had rejected Eli's way of life.

Points of interest
1. Samuel slept in the Sanctuary where the Covenant Box, the "Ark of the Covenant" was kept. This was a precious box which held the Ten Commandments. The Ark was later lost, probably when Israel was conquered by the Babylonians.

BELSHAZZAR'S FEAST
DANIEL: EPISODE 2
Daniel 5 ▶ *page 6*

A Christian perspective
Christians believe God communicates with the human race, whether that be for good or ill. In this case, God communicates his displeasure. Belshazzar's sins were overweening pride and the desecration of what was sacred. He saw himself as being so important that he could use, in a pagan feast, the cups that were only intended for use in worshipping God.

This story reflects Hebrew thinking: God, not self, should be the centre of a person's life. God knows all. He weighs people's actions. He can topple kings. Two famous prayers by Hannah (1 Samuel 2:1–10) and Mary (page 64) reflect this thinking.

"Stop your loud boasting; silence your proud words. For the Lord is a God who knows and he judges all that people do." (Hannah)

"He scatters the proud and puts down the mighty from their thrones." (Mary)

Points of interest
1. Belshazzar was the regent: his father, Nabonidus, had been away in Arabia for ten years. Belshazzar ruled the Babylonian Empire, the modern Iran/Iraq. This empire was taken over by the Medes and the Persians, as Daniel predicted.
2. The gifts Daniel was offered were royal gifts. Belshazzar may even have offered him a share in ruling the country.

THE PARABLE OF THE SOWER
Matthew 13.1–9, 18–23 ▶ *page 7*

A Christian perspective
This story is about the different ways in which the message is received. The story could be called the parable of the four soils. Despite all the obstacles, the farmer succeeds. The message takes root and grows. The field in this story stands for the world. The sower is Jesus.

Points of interest
1. This parable is one of the few that Jesus explained in detail. It is more like an allegory, for each part represents something else. Please see page 14 (Special Stories) for further details.
2. The land is very stony in parts of Palestine. This is a continual problem for the farmer.
3. In Palestine, the seed was often scattered before the land was ploughed.

GABRIEL'S MESSAGE
CHRISTMAS: EPISODE 1
Luke 1.26–45 ▶ *page 8*

A Christian perspective
In this story, God sends a message, via an angel, to Mary. Christians believe the son she had became a living message to the world about God. They believe that God sent his own son into the world to show what he is like. Jesus' life as well as his teachings became a living message.

Points of interest
1. The word "angel" simply means messenger. Angels have a long history in the Old Testament, often appearing as strangers.
2. In the Persian Empire there was a very fast postal route called the Royal Road. Stationed along it were changes of horses so that the king could quickly get a message to his people. The messengers of that service were called "angaros", a word that comes from the same word–root as the word "angels". Gabriel, like the Persian messengers, comes with a message — not from a king, but from The King.
3. Mary, or Miriam as her name would have been in Hebrew, was an ordinary girl. She was betrothed to Joseph. This was a legal ceremony which only death or divorce could break. Betrothal usually lasted about a year. The legal age for marriage was twelve for a woman, thirteen for a man. Mary could have been about fourteen, Joseph a little older.
4. Mary's pregnancy would have been construed as

proof of adultery by others. The penalty under Jewish Law was death. Jewish Law may not have been in force at this date. There was an option of private divorce in front of two witnesses, which Joseph was going to take before he was reassured that Mary had not committed adultery.

5. The name "Jesus" means "God saves". In Hebrew it is "Joshua".

Samuel Listens to God

1 Samuel 2.12–26; 3

Samuel snuggled back under the bedclothes. Was he hearing things? Twice he'd heard Eli calling him. He had got out of bed and hurried into the old man's room. Eli was very old and could not see very well, and Samuel was used to helping him. So he went quickly to see what was the matter. Well — he had thought it was the elderly priest calling him, but each time Eli had said it wasn't him. Had Samuel been dreaming? But the voice calling his name had been so clear. He turned over and tried to go to sleep — but there it was again! "Samuel! Samuel!"

It must be Eli. Who else would be calling him here in the Temple at night? He got up yet again, and went to the priest. "I'm here, Eli. You did call me!"

Eli sat up. What was the boy playing at? Then, suddenly, he knew what was happening. "Samuel," he explained, "it isn't me. It's God calling you. He has a message for you. If he calls you again, tell him you are ready to listen to him."

Eli watched the boy padding back to bed. Once, he thought enviously, God would have been speaking to me. That was before his sons had displeased God. They had been stealing the food the people brought for sacrifices, threatening the people with violence if it was not given to them straight away. Eli had known about it but he had not stopped them.

It had been a long while since Eli had heard God's voice. Poor Samuel! He looked so confused! He'd obviously never thought that such a thing could happen to him. It was rare now for God to speak to somebody in this way, for most people had stopped following and loving God.

The next morning, Eli watched Samuel closely. The boy seemed embarrassed: he hardly looked at Eli at all, and seemed reluctant to talk about the night before. Finally, Eli called him to him. He came at once, and Eli said, "What did God say to you last night, Samuel? You must not hide any part of the message from me, even if you think it will upset me."

Samuel looked at the old man. He really didn't want to give him God's message, but he knew he must. "I went back to bed, and did just as you told me to. When I heard God call my name again, I said, 'I'm here, Lord, listening. Tell me what you have to say.' God said that he is upset to see how people have been cheated by your sons. He says you did not stop them doing it, even though you knew it was wrong."

Eli nodded his head. He was not surprised at God's message. "He is our God," he said quietly. "He must do whatever he knows to be right."

God often spoke to Samuel during the next few years as he grew up in the Temple. He would bring God's messages for the people to them and teach them what God wanted them to do. Sometimes the messages were hard to give to the people, like his first one. Sometimes they made his listeners very angry with him. But whatever the message, Samuel passed each one on carefully to whomever God sent him to.

Belshazzar's Feast

DANIEL: EPISODE 2

Daniel 5

The tables were covered with rich and extravagant food from many countries and slaves rushed to and fro with more exotic dishes. King Belshazzar looked around the hall. His nobles were enjoying the banquet. "What a great and powerful king I am," he thought, "to be able to provide all this for a thousand people! Just look at all the food and wines!" Then he had an idea. "Bring in the gold and silver cups from Jerusalem, that Nebuchadnezzar captured in the Temple," he commanded. "Let's drink our wine from them!"

The guests thought this was a marvellous idea. "Just think," one of them said, as they lifted the cups full of wine, "the Israelites say their God is the true God, and here we are drinking out of the cups our gods helped us to take away from him!"

They all laughed, Belshazzar especially.

"They must realize now that I am even more powerful than that God of theirs!" he yelled.

Suddenly he stopped laughing. The people watching him saw him grow very pale. He gripped the edge of the table tightly: he could hardly stay upright. He was staring at the wall. What was it he saw? Then they saw it too. There, up on the wall, a human hand was moving. It was writing! What was happening? They were terrified. The king sent for his advisers.

"Quickly !" he shouted at them. "Tell me what those words mean. I'll make the man who does it rich and powerful."

But nobody could tell him. Belshazzar was even more frightened. What did the words mean? How could he do anything about them until he knew what they meant? The queen, hearing all the shouting and the bustle, came to see what was happening. When she saw the writing, she reminded Belshazzar about Daniel. "King Nebuchadnezzar considered him to be the wisest man in the land. Send for him." So Daniel was summoned to the king and the king offered him many gifts and great power if he would interpret the writing.

"I don't want your gifts," he told Belshazzar, "but with God's help, I will tell you what this means. Nebuchadnezzar was a great and powerful king. He knew that his power came from God. But you have made fun of God himself, and have boasted that your gods are stronger than the true and living God — your gods which are made of silver and gold and cannot even see or hear. So God has sent this message to you, Belshazzar. The message reads, '*Mene, Mene, Tekel Parsin.*' '*Mene*' means 'numbered': God is about to end your reign. Your days as king are numbered. '*Tekel*' means 'weighed': you have been weighed in God's balance of justice and have been found too light. You have failed to do right, and have done many evil things. '*Parsin*' means 'divided': God will divide your kingdom and give it to another."

And everything that Daniel had spoken of came true.

The Parable of the Sower

Matthew 13.1–9, 18–23

Once, so many people came to hear Jesus speak, that he had to go out a little way in a boat on the lake, so that they could all see him. He looked around at the countryside, beyond the crowds. Fishermen were working further around the lake and farmers were busy at their work. He saw the fields, full of crops, and began to tell a story about a man working in a field just like those he could see.

"A farmer set off one day to sow his wheat. He walked over his fields, scattering the small grains as he went. Not all of them fell on to the soil he had carefully prepared. Some of the grain fell on the well–trodden path through the field. The birds, always on the look out at sowing time, swooped down at once and quickly pecked up all the grains.

"Other grain fell on the rough patches at one side of the field, where the farmer had not yet had time to clear all the rocks. This grain grew because there were patches of soil among the rocks. It sprouted quickly, but its roots could not reach down very far into the earth, because of the rocks beneath it. So, when the sun grew hot, the little shoots shrivelled and died, for their roots could not reach down to the moisture which is hidden deep in the soil.

"Some of the wheat was scattered in the thorns along another edge of the field. These grains tried to grow, but the thorn plants were too strong. They took all the goodness and the moisture out of the soil, and crowded out the little wheat shoots, until they died.

"But most of the grain fell on the rich, prepared soil in the field. There, it grew strongly, until the farmer was able to harvest a heavy crop.

"Now think about this story and try to see what it is telling you."

Later Jesus explained the story to his disciples. Each part of it had a meaning.

"The grain is my teaching about God. The different places in which the seed falls, are the different kinds of people who hear the teaching. Sometimes, the word of God is taken away from people by the Devil, so that they don't even remember it. This is like the birds eating the grain off the path.

"Other people hear about God joyfully. They decide to follow him, and seem to be doing well. But they have no 'roots' — no real knowledge or love of God. As soon as difficulties arise, they stop trying to follow him. They are like the stony land, where the plants' roots cannot grow strong enough.

"Sometimes the love of money and of belongings, and the worries about everyday life, stop people following God — just as the thorns choked the young plants there. But the word of God often reaches 'good soil' — the hearts of people who want to follow him and who love him. They learn about God and obey him carefully. So they grow stronger all the time. They do his work among other people, and bring good to them with God's help, just as the wheat in the good soil of the field bears a good harvest."

Gabriel's Message

CHRISTMAS: EPISODE 1

Luke 1.26–45

Mary watched her baby as he slept, snug in the hay–filled trough. "He's so beautiful," she thought, stroking his cheek gently with her finger. "But then I expect all mothers think that!" She settled down on the bed of hay Joseph had collected for her. How her life had changed — and all in less than a year! Here she was in Bethlehem, miles from home, married, and with a tiny baby to care for.

She thought back to the day it had all started… just an ordinary day, spent in her usual jobs around the family home. But then a stranger had come up to her. She had been about to welcome him, when he had said, "Mary! God is with you and has greatly blessed you!"

Mary was surprised. This was an unusual way to start a conversation! Who was this man, bringing her a message from God? Was he one of God's own messengers — an angel? Why had he come to her? The stranger realized she was worried. "Don't be frightened," he told her. "God has been watching you, and he is pleased with all he has seen. He has a very special job for you to do for him. Very soon you will become pregnant, and you will have a baby son. You must call him Jesus, and he will be God's own son, as well as yours. He will be king over your people for ever."

"This is impossible," Mary thought. She took a deep breath and said to this messenger from God. "I'm not even married — only engaged, how can I have a baby?"

"Mary," he replied, "God himself will be the father of your baby. You will become pregnant through the power of the Holy Spirit. Now listen: Elizabeth, your cousin, is going to have a special baby, too. In fact, she's already six months pregnant and everyone believed that she was too old to have children. Remember, Mary, God can do anything."

Mary thought about her cousin. Elizabeth and Zechariah had always longed to have children and now they were going to have a baby! It was wonderful! If God could do this, then Mary knew she could trust him to look after her.

"Yes," she told the messenger. "I will do anything God wants me to do. Let it all happen, just as you have told me."

"And here I am," she thought now. "A mother, in a stable in a strange town. But God has looked after me. Joseph is such a good man, and we are very happy together. I know he'll look after Jesus as if he was his own child. But it's hard to believe that this is God's own son, while he's so small and helpless. God must trust us a great deal, to let us look after Jesus for him." She looked again at the small baby, and smiled across at Joseph, as he sat watching the baby, too.

RESOURCE BANK 3: MESSAGES FROM GOD

Graffiti Wall

Read the story called "Belshazzar's Feast" on page 6.

Group activity

Graffiti sprayed on walls ruins our environment and costs millions of pounds to clean up. This story is about a different sort of writing which appeared on a wall.

- Take a large sheet of paper. Divide the wall up into bricks with a felt pen. Using wax crayons held sideways, shade the bricks.

- Write on these bricks the sort of graffiti you might find on a wall (make sure it is suitable for school).

- Make a second wall and write on it the writing that appeared on the wall in the story of Belshazzar. If you wish, you can copy it in Hebrew.

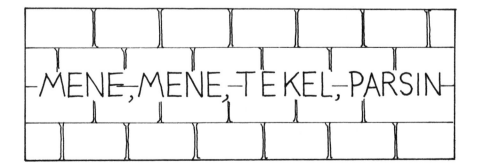

- As a group, prepare an assembly based on the story "Belshazzar's Feast". How could you use your two walls in your assembly? How could you bring out the difference between them? What point in the story would you try to communicate?

Messengers

Read the story on page 8.

The word "angel" means "messenger". Throughout the Bible, the angels bring messages to various people from God.

Five hundred years before Jesus was born, the Persians had a very fast postal service. There was a road stretching from the capital, where the king lived, to the coast. It was called the Royal Road. All along the road there were stations at which horses could be changed, so that a royal messenger leaving the palace could quickly reach the coast.

Angels, like the Persian royal messengers, brought messages from the "King". Christians call God the "King of Kings".

Activity

• Design a sheet of paper with a logo that indicates it comes from the king.

• On your sheet of paper, write Gabriel's message from God, whom Christians call the King, to Mary, a very ordinary girl.

Alliteration

Read the parable of the sower on page 7.

Alliteration is when two words start with the same sound, not necessarily the same letter.

Look at the poem below and mark the words in each line which start with the same sound.

> Softly the scattered seed sank to the earth,
> Some to be trampled beneath the tired feet of travellers,
> Some to be choked by the wild weeds of the wasteland.
> Others to rest in the shade of rugged rocks,
> Only to be scorched later by the merciless sun.
> But some lay buried in the rich brown earth
> and burst on a waiting world with golden grain.

This poem deliberately has lots of alliteration in it, so that you can see how it works. Alliteration can be very effective in a poem as long as it is not over used.

Activity

- Write your own poem on the parable of the sower, using some alliteration. You might like to choose just one seed and write what happened to it. For example: your poem could be about the seed that landed in the thorns, or the seed that was pecked by birds.

Important Messages

If you needed to send an important message quickly, how would you send it?

Activity

• Investigate the fastest and most reliable way of sending a message. How much would such a message cost to send?

• Look at the various messages sent in the stories on pages 5, 6, and 8.

Did they all come in the same way?
How many different means were used?

Think about it

Samuel, Mary, and Belshazzar had very unusual experiences.
Most Christians do not hear a voice, have writing appear on the wall, or see an angel. Christians believe God speaks in a variety of ways: he speaks through the Bible, through a quiet "voice" inside, or through other people and through circumstances.

SPECIAL STORIES OF JESUS

Understanding the biblical ideas

Jesus' stories are stories with a meaning. He said he would only teach the people using stories. Stories have many advantages:

- Stories make things easier to understand and remember.
- Stories are not just intellectual: they involve the imagination, which aids learning.
- Storytelling was a well tried and accepted method of teaching to which people were accustomed.
- Because it was not cerebral, it got past people's prejudices better than straight teaching. Can you imagine direct teaching on loving the enemy being as effective as the parable of the Good Samaritan?
- Stories often take time to "unpack": people can go away and think about them, so it is a less confrontational way of introducing new ideas.
- If people think through a story themselves and decide on the meaning, they "own" it far more than if it is imparted as teaching by someone else. It is a less passive process. Jesus did not often spell out the meaning of his parables: he left that to the hearers.

Many of Jesus' stories are called parables. Parables are literally "putting things side by side": they are a form of extended simile. The parable is often the only way in which Jesus could communicate his message of the kingdom because it could not be contained in more direct language. Jesus uses familiar images to communicate unfamiliar truths. The parable jolts people into looking at things in a new way. It calls for a decision about Jesus and the kingdom, since the parables are tied to the person of Jesus: they are not just about morality.

Introducing the passages

Start by exploring various stories with a meaning — Aesop's fables, modern parables. Look at stories such as C S Lewis's "Narnia" books (Fontana) or

Fay Sampson's "Finnglas" series (published by Lion). Picture books by authors such as Michael Foreman and David MacKee carry a meaning. These are short to read and the meaning is fairly easy to find.

Children can try telling their own stories with a meaning. Introduce some of Jesus' stories and work out the meaning with the children. Children might like to put some of the parables into modern form, but they have to be careful to keep the meaning the same.

Other useful passages

"The Good Samaritan", page 19.

"The Son Who left Home", Book 1, page 79–80.

"The Unforgiving Servant", Book 1, page 78.

"The Two Sons", Book 1, page 95.

"The Pharisee and the Tax Collector", page 63.

"The Unjust Judge and the Friend at Midnight", page 67.

"The Rich Fool", Book 1, page 63.

"The Parable of the Sower", page 7.

Cross–curricular links

Music

- Set the story of the Good Samaritan to music in the style of Prokofiev's *Peter and the Wolf*. Each character in this story has their own tune. Make up simple tunes for each character. The tune should reflect the character concerned. The book *Sing Song Roundabout — Bible Stories of Jesus* by B Piper and F Cooke (Longman) may be useful. (1)

Art

- Paint or crayon illustrations for a book which you have produced. (1)
- Choose a scene from any story in this section to produce an illustration in any medium for a new jacket for it. Invite an illustrator to come and discuss their work and how illustrations can enhance stories. (1)
- Look at the way stories were told in stained glass, in wall paintings and in tapestries. Use stained glass from the Middle Ages and the Victorian era. Look at frescoes depicting Bible stories such as Massachio's *Tribute Money* and tapestries by artists such as Burne Jones. (2)

Science and Technology

- Stories are an excellent basis for work in science and technology. The book *Technology from Stories* available from Hereford/Worcester Education Authority, Perdiswell I T Centre, Bilford Road, Worcester is an excellent source for ideas. Jesus' stories such as the Two Houses and the Sower also have possibilities tor technology and science.

English

- Read a biblical story and write a book review for it. (2, 3)
- Write a précis of a story as part of a jacket for a book — it could be for your own story, for an old favourite, or one of Jesus' stories. (3)

- Make a tape of your story with appropriate sound effects. (1) (Mu 1)
- Visit the local newspaper offices and find out how a story is developed from the initial idea right through to the finished product. How many times is it redrafted, edited, etc…? Who has the final word on the finished article? (1, 3)
- Dramatize the parable of the Great Feast. (1)
- Set up a "Chat Show": interview the main characters in the parable of the Good Samaritan and question them concerning their behaviour. (1, 3)

Mathematics

- Investigate the cost of producing one of the stories in this section as a story book. Write to a publisher and ask for some facts and figures. (1, 2)
- Cost what it would take to publish a four–page story of your own. How much would you need to charge to cover your costs? (2)

History

- Look at medieval miracle plays and how these were used to tell Bible stories. Adapted versions of these can be found in *Miracle Plays* by A Malcolmson (Constable). These plays were still performed in Tudor times and can be looked at under the unit "Tudors and Stuarts". (1, 2, 3)
- In early history, stories were passed down by word of mouth. Find out when printing began and books became more accessible. Find out about early forms of story writing. What kinds of writing materials were available at different stages in the development of writing? Make a zig–zag book to show your research into the main ones. (1, 2, 3) (EAT 2, 3)

PE/Dance

- Perform part of a mystery/miracle play for the class. (KS 2)
- Use mime for the story of the Two Houses. (KS 1/2)

THE SHEEP AND THE GOATS

Matthew 25.31–46 ▶ *page 18*

A Christian perspective

In this story, Jesus accepts love expressed to those in need as offered to himself. This is in line with the Old Testament in which an offering to God could be made via the poor. Love expressed in a practical way to those in need was accepted as love expressed to God. In this story, people are judged by how they have expressed their relationship with God practically. The loving actions should be the result of the relationship. Judgement is expressed in this story as being with God or being excluded from his presence. The Bible describes heaven as the place where God is. Hell is being apart from God.

Points of interest

1. Sheep and goats were normally kept together in Israel at this time (and still are).

2. The actions described are basic humanitarian behaviour. Food and water are the basics of life. Clothes are for warmth and dignity. The Jews saw nakedness as undignified. Middle Eastern hospitality meant the stranger should have been welcomed. Those who were sick or in prison needed support if they had no family to look after them.

THE GOOD SAMARITAN
Luke 10.25–37 ▶ *page 19*

A Christian perspective

The point of the story is that the Samaritan behaved in a ridiculously generous manner. The priest and Levite behaved in a perfectly reasonable manner. How could they know it was not a trap? They may have thought the man dead, and therefore avoided contact with him, as contact with the dead made them ceremonially unclean. This would mean they would not have been able to carry out their duties at the Temple. The person who asked, "Who is my neighbour?" wanted a nice, legal definition. Jesus made him think differently by asking whom he would have wanted as a neighbour, had he been the injured man.

Points of interest

1. The Samaritans and the Jews were enemies. Often a Jew would detour rather than walk through Samaritan territory. This enmity had historical roots. The Samaritans were not regarded as pure in race or worship by the Jews. Several hundred years previously, the Jews had excluded the Samaritans from rebuilding the walls and the Temple in Jerusalem. This increased the bad feeling. In answer, the Samaritans built their own temple on Mount Gerizim, which the Jews later destroyed.
2. The Levite was a helper at the Temple, as was the priest.
3. The road between Jericho and Jerusalem, the Wadi Qelt, is a deserted area through which travellers did not usually venture alone. It is steep, descending 3,000 ft in seventeen miles.
4. The man paid the innkeeper two silver coins, two denarii. This was the equivalent of two days' wages. It is uncertain how long a stay at the inn this would have paid for.
5. The man's wounds were bound up with oil and wine, standard treatment for the age. The wine had a certain antiseptic value. The oil may have been used to prevent the bandages sticking.

THE GREAT FEAST
Luke 14.15–24 ▶ *page 20*

A Christian perspective

In this parable, Jesus offers the Kingdom to the people in society who were normally rejected. He is throwing the doors wide open. Christians believe he never turns anyone away.

The people invited first stand for the Jews, particularly the religious leaders. They are invited first, but if they will not come others will be invited. Although the Jewish leaders are here singled out for criticism, it must be remembered that the bulk of Jesus' followers were Jewish.

Points of interest

1. The excuses given were all reasonable ones. Men who had just married or who had not ploughed their land were all excused military service. The point is that the guests underestimated the importance of the invitation. This feast was more important than war!
2. Heaven is often likened to a great banquet.

THE LOST COIN AND THE LOST SHEEP
Luke 15.1–10 ▶ *page 21*

A Christian perspective

For Christians, these stories express God's joy at welcoming back a person he has "lost". The emphasis is on joy and forgiveness. The lost coin and sheep represent people who are far away from God. The shepherd was a symbol of a loving God.

Points of interest

1. A man with a hundred sheep was moderately well off. The other sheep would not have been abandoned, they would probably have been left in the care of a hired helper.
2. The coin was a drachma, approximately the same as a denarius which was a day's wage. Someone who only owned ten drachmae would be quite poor. It may have been part of the coin headdress some married women wore, though it does not say that in the story.
3. Houses were dark with small windows high up. The search would have been difficult.

PARABLES OF THE KINGDOM
Matthew 13.31–33, 44–46 ▶ *page 22*

A Christian perspective

These four parables, or stories are about the Kingdom of God. In Christian thinking, the Kingdom of God is not so much a place, as the people whom God rules. The Kingdom spreads as each new person accepts God as their king.

The parables of "The Mustard Seed" and "The Yeast" express the quiet growth of the Kingdom and its small beginnings. The parables of "The Pearl" and "The Treasure" express the value of the Kingdom and the person's joy at finding it.

Points of interest

1. Money was often buried. In the days before banks, burial in the ground was the safest way of storing money. It is this habit which has led to so many "finds" by archaeologists.
2. The mustard bush provided a vegetable as well as flavouring. The growth of the Kingdom is likened to the growth potential of the seed. The shrub grows to about three metres high.
3. Pearls were of great worth in the ancient world. Merchants from the Middle East would go as far as India looking for them.

The Sheep and the Goats

Matthew 25.31–46

Jesus told some of his stories to illustrate what would happen when he returned to the earth as king. This is one of those stories.

"Look at that flock over there. It's hard to tell from here which are the sheep and which are the goats. Until the farmer needs to separate them for some reason, the two kinds of animals live together, eat together, and rest together, quite happily! It's like that with people. You all live together in your villages or towns, but you are not all the same. Some people are good, others are not.

"I am like a shepherd, and people are like a mixed flock of sheep and goats. One day I will separate the sheep from the goats. To one group I will say: 'God is pleased with you. You can now live with him and with me for ever. For when I was thirsty you gave me water. You gave me food when I was hungry, and clothes to wear when I needed them. You welcomed me as a stranger, visited me in prison, nursed me when I was ill.'

"The people in this first group will look at each other in surprise. 'But we didn't do any of these things for you!' they'll say. But I will tell them that they did — because they cared for other people in these ways, and so showed their love of me in action.

"But to the other people I will say, 'Go away from me. God is not pleased with you. For when I was thirsty you gave me no water. You gave me no food when I was hungry, and no clothes to wear when I needed them. You did not welcome me when I was a stranger, you never visited me in prison, or nursed me when I was ill.'

"The people in this second group, too, will look at each other in surprise. 'But we never saw you cold, thirsty nor hungry. We never saw you ill or in prison. Neither did we meet you as a stranger!' they'll say. But I will tell them that they did — because every time they failed to care for other people in these ways, they failed to care for me."

The Good Samaritan

Luke 10.25–37

Jesus was talking to a crowd of people one day when one of them asked him, "What should I do to please God?"

"You know what to do: it is written in the Law," Jesus replied.

"Yes: love God, and love and care for your neighbour as yourself. But who is my neighbour?"

"I'll tell you," Jesus said. "Listen to this." And he told them this story.

"A man once set off to walk from Jerusalem to Jericho. As you know, robbers often lie in wait for travellers on that road. Sure enough, before he had gone very far, the man was attacked. The robbers beat him up, and stole his belongings and clothes. They left him lying in the dust, half–dead. The sun burned down on him, and it seemed he would die there alone.

"Then a man walked round a bend in the road. It was a priest!" Some of Jesus' listeners nodded their heads wisely: the man would be saved now.

"But," Jesus went on, "when the priest caught sight of the man lying there, he quickly crossed the road. He held his robe tightly against his legs, and hurried past as quickly as he could.

"Still the man lay there, just alive. Another traveller approached. This time it was a Levite. But he didn't go over to the injured man either. Perhaps he was afraid he would be attacked as well. He rushed past, nervously checking the hillside and rocks above the road.

"Finally, a third man, riding a donkey, came into sight. Would he help? But he was a Samaritan."

The crowd sighed. Well, the man would surely die now. A Samaritan would never help a Jew, would he? Poor man! But what was Jesus saying?

"The Samaritan got off his donkey and hurried over to the man. He carefully bandaged his injuries, talking to him quietly. He lifted him on to his donkey and led him further along the road, to an inn. There he settled the injured man comfortably in bed. 'Take this money,' he said to the innkeeper. 'Make sure this man has everything he needs until he is well enough to go home. If you spend more than this, I'll pay you next time I'm here.'

"Now," Jesus asked the man who had questioned him, "who acted as a neighbour to that man — the priest, the Levite, or the Samaritan?"

Reluctantly, the man gave the only answer he could give. "The Samaritan, of course, because he cared for him."

"That's right," Jesus told him. "Now you go and behave like that — looking after people, whoever they are."

The Great Feast

Luke 14.15–24

A man once decided to give a great feast for his friends. He sent out all the invitations in plenty of time. Then he carefully planned the meal, buying the best of everything. He was very busy on the day of the feast, making sure that all the food was perfectly cooked and very tasty.

At last he was satisfied — but where were the guests? "Perhaps they've forgotten the date or the time," he thought. He sent out his servant to tell his friends to hurry, or the food would spoil! But the servant came back alone. Every one of his friends had made some excuse.

"But I've only just got married. I can't come now," said one.

One said, "I've just bought a new field. I'll have to go and inspect it at once."

And yet another explained that he must try out his new oxen in harness!

The man was furious! After all his work and the care he had taken to please them! He sent out the servant again. "Go into all the back streets and alleys of the town," he ordered. "Bring back with you all the poor people you can find, and all the lame or blind people who have to beg for their money."

So the servant hurried away and did this. But still there were empty places at the tables, next to the new guests — who sat there very happily but also in some amazement!

"Go out again," the man ordered, "out into the countryside. Bring back anyone who is willing to come. We must fill up all the places. But remember: not one of my original guests is to come."

RESOURCE BANK 3: SPECIAL STORIES OF JESUS

The Lost Sheep and the Lost Coin

Luke 15.1–10

All kinds of people enjoyed listening to Jesus. Some of the religious leaders complained about this. "He even welcomes tax collectors and other people who have done many wrong things," they muttered.

Jesus knew what they were saying, so he told these two stories to show that every single person is important to God — even if other people do not think they are worth anything.

"A man once owned a hundred sheep. He would often count them while he was looking after them out on the hills. He didn't want to lose any of them, they were all valuable to him.

"One day, he realized that one of them was missing. He had only counted up to ninety–nine! What should he do? 'I'll just have to leave these sheep here, where they are safe, and go to look for the other one,' he thought, and he set off on his search. He went back over the path they had taken that day, checking in briar patches and behind rocks. Where was that sheep? It was worth a lot to him: he must find it.

"At last he spotted it. He talked to it quietly, so that it wouldn't run off. The sheep was glad to see him: it recognized his voice and came up to him. The man picked it up. Carrying the sheep across his shoulders, he hurried back to his house. He was so pleased to have all the sheep home safely, that he called all his friends over to his house for a party.

"That is what happens when each man becomes a friend of God," Jesus explained. "God and all his angels are happy and celebrate together, because each person is worth a lot to God. He does not want even one person to be lost."

Jesus also told this story.

"God is like the woman in this story. The woman had ten silver coins. They were her most valuable possession. She loved to look at them, gleaming in the light, and she took great care of them. One day she realized that one coin was missing. Where could it be?

"She quickly lit a lamp to help her and began to search. She searched all over the floor, carefully sweeping out all the dark corners and awkward angles. She gently shook out the bedding, listening for the 'chink' which would tell her where the coin fell. She searched among her pots and pans. Then, as she turned round with the lamp in her hand, her eyes caught a tiny flash of light, over near the door. She rushed over, bent down — and yes, it was the coin, glinting in the lamplight! She called to her friends, 'Come on, let's celebrate. I've found my coin!'"

Parables of the Kingdom

The Mustard Seed *Matthew 13.31–33*

The mustard seed is one of the smallest seeds you can find. Yet, when it is planted, it grows into one of the biggest plants in the garden, so big that birds can perch on its branches to find shelter from the sun. It is like this with the Kingdom of Heaven. It starts from small beginnings — in a person who begins to follow Jesus, or in a country where a few followers work together — but with God's power it grows and grows.

The Yeast *Matthew 13.33*

When you make bread you take a little yeast and mix it with large amounts of flour, oil, and water. You need only a little yeast and it can raise large amounts of dough. In the same way, God's Kingdom starts in a small way but it can affect many.

The Pearl *Matthew 13.45–46*

Jesus told two stories to explain how important the Kingdom of God was. This is what he said:

Imagine a merchant who has spent years searching for fine pearls to buy and sell. One day, he finds a wonderful pearl, by far the most beautiful and most valuable he has ever seen. He rushes home and sells everything he has, just so that he can buy this one beautiful pearl.

The Treasure *Matthew 13.44*

It is also like a man who, when he is working in someone else's field, finds a treasure hidden there. He quickly buries it again. He finds out how much the field would cost him, and then he sells everything to raise that much money. But he knows it is worth doing, because there is treasure in that field. So, a man who has become a follower of God is willing to make any sacrifice, because God's friendship is worth far more than anything else.

Stories in Glass

Before ordinary people could go to school and learn to read, most people learned Jesus' stories by hearing them read out loud, by watching them acted out in drama, or by seeing them painted on church walls or pictured in stained–glass windows. If you have a local church which has stained–glass windows or wall paintings, you might like to visit the church with your teacher or parents.

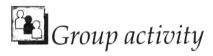 *Group activity*

- How could you make a stained–glass window which you could use to tell one of the stories of Jesus? Each group should put their suggestions on paper and then the class should vote on the various designs. When you have made your decision, select one of Jesus' stories to tell in art.

Miracle Plays

Many of Jesus' stories were told as miracle plays in the Middle Ages. Miracle plays started as Bible readings with short pieces of drama. They grew and grew until eventually they had to be moved outside the church. Here is a short extract from a miracle play (Anne Malcolmson, *Miracle Plays,* Constable, 1960).

The Nativity (York Cycle)
We have sought both up and down,
Through diverse streets of this city!
So many people are come to town
That we can find no hostelry.
There is such a rabble,
Forsooth, no other help I see
But this poor stable.

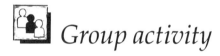

Group activity

- In a group turn one of Jesus' stories into a short play.

Think about it

Why do you think people found the stories easier to remember as plays?

The Yeast

Read the stories called "Parables of the Kingdom" on page 22.

Jesus said the Kingdom of God was like yeast. The amount of yeast you use in breadmaking is tiny but it can make a large amount of dough rise.

Activity

- Using a basic bread recipe, test out this parable with the help of an adult.

- Follow the instructions for making your bread until you get to the point where you leave it to rise.

- Work out a way of measuring how much the mixture rises due to the yeast. Make sure any method you use is safe and hygienic.

Think about it

Yeast is tiny but has great potential growth. In the same way, Christians believe that the Kingdom, or family of God starts small, but steadily grows.

Can you think of another way to explain this idea of something starting small and growing large.

Lost and Found

Imagine you have lost some money.
Where would you look?
How would you look?

Activity for two

• Mime losing something which is very precious to you.

  Jesus told three "lost and found" stories.
  The lost coin, page 21.
  The lost sheep, page 21.
  The lost son (The Son Who Left Home), Book 1, page 80.

• Read each story. Choose one of them to present as a dramatized reading.

• While one person reads the story, the other silently mimes what is happening.

Think about it

What message was Jesus trying to communicate in these "lost" parables?

JESUS 1

Understanding the biblical ideas

For Christians, Jesus is more than a good man. They believe he is the Son of God. The teachings of Jesus cannot be separated from his miracles, or his claims concerning who he was. For example: after the healing of a blind man, Jesus talks about himself as being the light of the world.

Jesus' healings were not just stunts which he performed to make people believe in him. That temptation he refused. He often told people to keep quiet about the healings. These healings were done out of compassion, and as part of the general defeat of evil that was the purpose of his life, death, and resurrection.

Christians believe Jesus shared our human existence, but with one difference: he did no wrong. Jesus was baptized by John the Baptist, but as an example and act of solidarity, rather than as an act of repentance.

Jesus is seen as the Christ or Messiah, the promised king sent by God. Jesus accepted this title but redefined it. This Christ achieved his ends by suffering, not by violence or political power.

Jesus claimed to be the Son of God, a claim that finally earned him the death sentence. He also called himself Son of Man, an unusual title to which he gave his own meaning. This title stressed his humanity, but it was also a title that was used of the coming judge of the earth.

Jesus described himself in a number of ways: light, bread, gate, shepherd, etc. Each of these reveals a little more about his character and role.

Introducing the stories

Dirty a clean T–shirt with chalk and wash it. Discuss getting things clean using water. Talk about water as a symbol of getting clean on the inside. Just as water washes away the things that spoil clothes, so Christians believe God can help people get rid of the things that spoil life. Baptism is an outward way of demonstrating that inward cleansing. Introduce the story of Jesus' baptism.

Set up some case studies in which people are tempted to do wrong. Explore with the children what the characters might be tempted to do. Read the story of Jesus' temptation. Set up situations in which shop keepers start cheating and giving the wrong change. Introduce the story of "Jesus and the Money Changers".

Talk about where people like to pray. What would praying in the middle of a market be like?

Play the metaphor game. "If I were a colour, I would be…" "If I were a tree, I would be…" "If I were a food, I would be…"

Example: if Peter were a colour, he'd be bright orange. If he were food, he would be a beefburger. Introduce Jesus' "I am" sayings which use metaphor.

Other useful passages

The section entitled "Jesus 2", pages 47–52.

The section entitled "Special Stories of Jesus", pages 18–22.

Other stories told by Jesus can be found on pages 7, 63, 67; Book 1, pages 63, 78, 79–80, 95, 99.

Miracles performed by Jesus can be found in: Book 1, pages 8, 95; Book 1, pages 7, 10, 22, 35, 51–52, 81; Book 2, pages 34, 63, 105, 106, 107.

The teaching of Jesus can be found on pages 62, 97; Book 1, pages 36, 37, 68–69, 83; Book 2, pages 19, 20, 22.

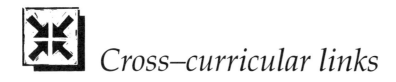

Cross–curricular links

English
- Invite people from local churches to come and talk about the "I Am" sayings and what they think they mean. Prepare questions prior to the visit. Write formal letters of invitation. (Please choose the people you invite with care. They need to be people who understand the school context and can speak to children.) (1, 3)
- Think about preparations a Christian family would need to make to celebrate a family baptism. List the preparations and when each item needs organizing, perhaps in diary form. Look at Jesus' metaphors — "I am the light, bread, gate, shepherd", etc. Look at common metaphors "You're a brick". (1, 2, 3)

Mathematics
- What is a census? Collect data for your family, collate and make graphs or make a database on the computer (be sensitive over this). (5)
- Look at catalogues, and plan suitable baptism gifts for a young baby, toddler. (1, 2)
- Do some exercises in changing money, giving change and exchange rates. (2)

Geography
- Think about Mary and Joseph's journey from Nazareth to Bethlehem — build a large three–dimensional table–top map of the Holy Land putting flags in to mark various places, etc. Use the map in connection with Bible stories in this section. (1)

Music
- Look at hymns which reflect the stories in this section, such as "Ride on, Ride on, in Majesty," and "Forty Days and Forty Nights", both of which may be found in Songs of Praise (OUP). How much of the story can you detect from the hymns? (2)

Science
- Link Jesus' saying "I am the light of the world" with the candle sometimes given at Christian baptism. Investigate the different properties of light and link these with Jesus' saying where appropriate. (1, 4)

Technology
- Design and make a card for a Christian adult or a baby to celebrate their baptism. Think carefully about an appropriate picture. (1, 2)
- Look at how the different beliefs concerning baptism affect the design of church buildings. Try to build your own church using a construction kit, e.g. Lego. (1, 2)

Art
- Make simple puppets to tell some of the story of the temptation. (1)
- Make palm crosses. (1)
- Create a symbol for each of the "I am" sayings. Make the symbol simple enough to be printed. (1)
- Use batik to create candle designs. (1)

PE/Dance
- Explore different ways of welcoming people in dance. (KS 1/2)
- Make up a dance of triumph to the "Ode to Joy" at the end of Beethoven's Ninth Symphony, "Nessum Dorma" by Puccini or "Chariots of Fire" by Vangelis to express joy at the entry of Jesus into Jerusalem. (KS 1/2)

History
- Put the story of Jesus in its Roman context. This can become part of the background for the "Invaders and Settlers" unit, looking at the Romans in detail. (1, 2, 3)

JESUS IS BAPTIZED
Matthew 3.13–17 ▶ *page 31*

A Christian perspective
Jesus was baptized, though Christians believe it was not necessary as they believe that he did nothing wrong. People were baptized to show they were sorry for things they had done wrong and wanted a fresh start with God. Jesus was baptized as an example to others and to identify with ordinary people.

John was the forerunner of Jesus. Christians see him as the one who prepared the people to receive Jesus' message. The Old Testament predicted that Elijah would return before the Messiah. Jesus said that John was that Elijah figure, come to prepare the way for the special king

Points of interest
1. Water was a symbol of cleansing, an outward sign of the washing away of wrong. John the Baptist was not the only person to use baptism. It was used by other groups such as the Essenes who were a group of strict Jews who lived in the area of the Dead Sea.

2. The dove is a symbol of the Holy Spirit. At creation the Spirit is described as "hovering" over the waters. It was also used as a symbol of Israel.
3. The voice of God is called the Bath Qol. Literally it means "daughter of a voice". Whether only Jesus heard a voice, or whether others heard it as well, is not clear from the text.

JESUS IS TEMPTED
Luke 4.1–13 ▶ *page 32*

A Christian perspective
Christians believe Jesus suffered from the temptation to do wrong the same as anyone else. He had a job to do and he had to decide which way to do it. He had great powers, but how would he use them? He chose the path of suffering and obedience. The first temptation was to use his powers to feed himself. He could also have used them to get quick popularity by feeding the people. Although Jesus did use his powers to feed people occasionally, he did not use them to buy cheap popularity. The second temptation was to serve evil, which Jesus refutes, as only God is to be worshipped. The third temptation was to perform a stunt, which would compel people to believe in him. It would also force God's hand. Jesus refuses to do this. When Jesus did perform miracles, he generally required faith first, either on the part of the person or someone committed to them. In this way the miracle happened within a relationship. He did not perform tricks in order to make people believe.

The temptations may have been thoughts originating from an evil source, called the Devil or Satan in the Bible. This is evil personified, evil with a will and purpose. It has nothing to do with the comic figure in red tights!

JESUS THE KING
Mark 11.1–11 ▶ *page 33*

A Christian perspective
In this entry to Jerusalem and in accepting the people's public praise, Christians believe Jesus was announcing that he was the special king or Messiah. By the way in which he entered the city, and by the events of the next week, he was to reshape the people's idea of the special king from a "warrior" to a "suffering servant".

Points of interest
1. The ass or donkey was the usual mode of travel. Horses were used by kings and for war. The crowd called out "Hosanna" — "save now". Jesus' name means "God saves". They also called him "Son of David": the special king they were waiting for, the Messiah, was to be a descendant of David.
2. Coats were valuable. They were the poor person's blanket as well as the outer garment. They were not lightly put on the ground.
3. The religious leaders may have been hostile because they feared a revolt and they did not want Roman interference. They may also have been jealous of Jesus' popularity.
4. The Romans were particularly nervous about riots at religious festivals. They thought the Jews were a volatile people so they had their fortress, Antonia, next to the Temple so that they could quash any riot quickly.

JESUS AND THE MONEYCHANGERS
Mark 11.15–19 ▶ *page 34*

A Christian perspective
Jesus assumes an authority in the Temple which no ordinary person had. Like the entry into Jerusalem, it was the act of a king, the Messiah. Christians believe Jesus was the Messiah or special king and therefore had a right to clear the moneychangers out of the Temple. The Temple was the place in which people could meet with God in a special way, though the Jews never made the mistake of thinking that God lived there.

Points of interest
1. A subsidiary theme in this story is honesty and deceit. Jesus threw out the cheating money–changers because such behaviour was an affront to a God of truth. It also meant that the only place non–Jews (Gentiles) had to worship God was taken up by a market. Non–Jews were not allowed beyond the area called "The Court of the Gentiles". There were notices warning that Gentiles who crossed into the Jewish Courts could incur the death penalty.
2. Moneychangers changed ordinary money into special Temple money. Ordinary Roman money could not be used because it had Caesar's head on it. Caesar claimed to be a god, so the coins could not be brought into the Temple because their presence would have been highly offensive to the Jews.

3. Three times a year, Jews came up to Jerusalem. Animals for sacrifice were kept to sell to these pilgrims. Jesus not only objected to the cheating that went on, he objected to a place of prayer being turned into a market.

THE I AM SAYINGS
John 6.35; 8.12; 10.7, 10, 11, 14; 11.25; 14.6; 15.1 ▶ *page 35*

A Christian perspective

Jesus likens himself to bread, the staple diet of the poor. Bread was the sustainer of life. Just as God provided manna in the desert for the children of Israel, so Christians believe he provided Jesus as a different sort of "bread". Bread gives ordinary life: Jesus gives a different sort of life — a new life in friendship with God.

The "door" or "gate" was the legitimate entrance. Thieves would climb over the wall and steal. The shepherd lay across the entrance to protect the sheep, and literally became the door. Just as a door is a way through to another place, so Jesus said he was the way to find the Father.

The "good shepherd" is contrasted with the hired hands, who had a bad reputation. The shepherd knows his sheep (people) individually and many eastern shepherds still do. A good shepherd stayed to defend the sheep, the hired hand tended to run away.

Light was a valuable commodity. Light guides, light reveals — like the lights left on in shop windows at night. The light referred to here is the light of truth and the light that shows the way.

Jesus called himself the "resurrection and the life". This was spoken in the context of the raising of Lazarus. Jesus gives Lazarus new life. Christians believe that friendship with Jesus survives death.

Jesus called himself "the vine". In a plant, the branches have no source of life in themselves: to live they have to stay close to the parent vine. Christians similarly have to stay close to Jesus.

Jesus describes himself as the "way" to the Father. The way is about destination, the destination being God. He also describes himself as "the truth". This means he is the one who speaks the truth about God. He is called "the life" because Christians believe he is the source of a new life with God.

Jesus is Baptized

Matthew 3.13–17

Down by the River Jordan, a group of people was listening to John the Baptist. He was asking them to say sorry to God for all the times they had disobeyed God's Laws. He spoke about God's longing to forgive them all, telling them that he, John, would baptize them in the river, as a sign that God had made them clean from their wrong deeds, just as the water of the river washed over them and cleaned their bodies.

Suddenly, John stopped speaking and looked up. A man was walking towards them. He seemed to be just an ordinary man, but John knew at once that he was special. John had often told the people about the special king whom God would send to them. This man, the Christ, would bring people into friendship with God. Now here he was coming to John and asking to be baptized!

"You do not need to be baptized!" John answered, because he knew that Jesus had never made God unhappy by doing wrong.

But Jesus gently corrected him, "Yes, you must baptize me," for Jesus knew that it was the right thing to do.

So John baptized him. As Jesus rose up out of the river, with water streaming off his hair and clothes, the Spirit like a dove came down and settled on him — a sign that God's Spirit was with him, and God's voice said, "This is my dear Son. I am very pleased with him."

John turned to the people around them. "God has told me that this man is the one I said would come to you. He will take away all our sins."

So Jesus, helped by the Holy Spirit, began to prepare for the special work he was to do for God for the next three years.

Jesus is Tempted

Luke 4.1–13

As soon as Jesus had been baptized, he went out into the wild, empty desert, to be alone with God, and to decide just how he was going to do the job he had come to do. And while he was in the desert, he was tempted by the devil.

Jesus did not eat while he was there. He wanted to do nothing but talk and listen to God. The Devil knew Jesus was very hungry. He also knew that Jesus was determined not to give in to him. "I can defeat him through his hunger," he thought craftily.

"Jesus!" he said to him. "You're very hungry. Why don't you turn all these stones into bread? You know you could do it — and who else would know?"

But Jesus was ready for him. "Never! Food isn't the most important thing. It's more important for a person to obey God, than just to have food to eat."

So the Devil tried again. "Come with me, Jesus," he said, and led him to the top of a high hill. "Look! All those lands you can see! Think of all their riches! You can own them all. I'll give them all to you. All you have to do is to bow down to me and worship me. Just treat me as your god and I'll give them to you."

Jesus knew what to say to this. He knew that the Devil was lying as usual. "The Law tells us that we are to worship only the Lord, the true God!" he retorted.

But still the temptations came. How easy it would be to give in! Jesus was tired and hungry, dreading some of the events he knew must come in the future. And the Devil knew this. He took Jesus to the very top of the great Temple in Jerusalem. "Prove that you are the Son of God!" he taunted. "Throw yourself down from here. If you really are his son, God himself will send his angels to protect you from injury. They will catch you safely!"

This was hard! Jesus knew he was God's son, that he was the only one who could help all these people — and he knew that he must die in order to do that.

"No!" he shouted triumphantly at the Devil. "It is written in the Law that we mustn't test God like that."

And the Devil gave up for a time. "I'll try again, when he's tired and frightened and alone," he thought, and he left him.

Jesus was ready to begin his work. He knew who he was, and he knew that he had great power. But he now knew how he was to use that power. He was not to use that power to stun people into believing him. Neither was he to use it to get popularity. No, he was to tread the long, hard road of suffering.

RESOURCE BANK 3: JESUS 1

Jesus the King

Mark 11.1–11

In the crowded streets of Jerusalem, the news spread rapidly. "Jesus is coming! He's coming into the city!" Nearly everyone there had heard about some of the amazing things that Jesus had done. Many of them wanted to see him again. Some lined the streets on the way to the Temple, impatiently waiting for him. Others rushed out of the city gate to meet Jesus on his way. There, riding along the dusty road was Jesus. His disciples were around him excitedly waving the branches they'd snapped off the palm trees. Many in the crowd joined in with them. "Hosanna!" they cried. "Blessed is the King of Israel! Hosanna!" They threw down their cloaks in front of Jesus to make a royal road for him. So Jesus entered Jerusalem, riding through the gate.

Many there must have been puzzled when they saw him. They had hoped that here was the special king, the Messiah they had waited for, the Messiah who would call them to battle and defeat the Romans who now ruled over them. It was Passover time and the city was crowded with people who had come up for the festival. When these people heard Jesus was here, in Jerusalem, and heard the cries of the crowd, and saw the palm branches waving over his head, they must have believed that he had come as their king, to lead them to victory and freedom at last.

But this was no war leader they saw coming towards them. This was an ordinary man, riding not on a war horse, but on a young donkey which his disciples had borrowed for him. He had no flowers or rich carpets to ride on, only the cloaks of his followers, thrown in the dust. His companions were not war captains, and he was followed by no army: they were just men who had seen and heard so many wonderful things that their love and admiration of Jesus now spilled over into praise. For Jesus was entering Jerusalem as its true king and he was going to rule over a kingdom built by God's love, not by war.

Jesus and the Moneychangers

Mark 11.15–19

The Courts of the Temple were even busier than usual that day. So many people had come to Jerusalem to celebrate the feast of the Passover, and to worship in the Temple. The men selling animals to the people to use in their worship were very happy. They had to keep bringing in more animals, they were selling so many. They could charge whatever they liked. The people had to buy animals and most of them did not know what the usual price was, anyway. The moneychangers were well satisfied too. The Jews coming from other countries had to change their own currency into that used here. What did it matter if the changers did not give them quite what their own coins were worth? The foreigners would never know the difference! So, business went on much as usual — until Jesus arrived.

Jesus stood watching all the people milling about in the Courts. He saw the cheating and the greed: he saw poor people being robbed. And he thought about how this place should look — how God wanted his special Temple to be. Jesus was angry. He began to throw over the tables of the moneychangers, with their piles of coins. He upset the baskets holding the doves. He chased out the larger animals, the sheep and the cows. He drove out the stallholders. "This is my Father's house, not a den for thieves!" he shouted. "How dare you use God's Temple like this? Get out of here!"

The disciples watched him. They realized how hurt and angry he was — and with good reason. But his enemies were watching him too. The Jewish leaders were far from pleased to have Jesus interfering with their Temple like this. In any case, he was becoming far too popular with the people.

The I Am Sayings

I am the bread of life
Anyone who comes to me will never be hungry and anyone who believes in me will never go thirsty. (John 6.35)

I am the door of the sheepfold
Anyone who enters by me will find a new life, for I have come so that people may have life in all its fullness. (John 10.7, 10)

I am the good shepherd
The good shepherd lays down his life for the sheep. I know my sheep and my sheep know me, and I lay down my life for the sheep. (John 10.11, 14)

I am the light of the world
Anyone who follows me will never walk in darkness, but have the light of life. (John 8.12)

I am the resurrection and the life
Anyone who believes in me will live, even though they die. (John 11.25)

I am the vine and you are the branches
If a person remains in me and I in them, they will bear much fruit. (John 15.1,5)

I am the way, the truth, and the life
No one comes to the Father except through me. (John 14.6)

Temptation

Read the story "Jesus is Tempted" on page 32.

C S Lewis wrote a book called *The Screwtape Letters* (Fount, 1982). In it were letters from an imaginary older devil to a younger one. The younger devil, called Screwtape, was out on his first temptation practice, and the older devil, who was called Wormwood, wrote some letters offering him advice. Here is the type of advice Uncle Wormwood gave:

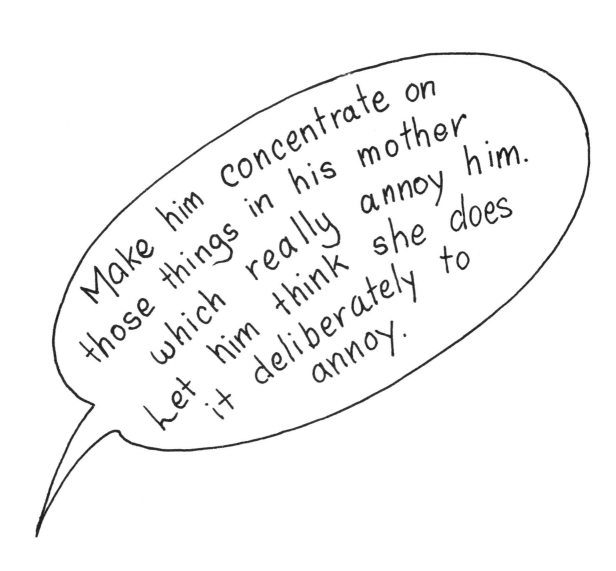

Group activity

Imagine a person has found a ten pound note on the floor. Pretend she is the human on whom Screwtape is practising. What advice do you think Uncle Wormwood would have given young Screwtape: what would he have told Screwtape to whisper in her ear?

Temptation is like a battle that goes on inside. Whatever ideas people have of the devil, the important point of Christian belief is that there is a force for evil which tempts people to do wrong. Christians believe Jesus was tempted just as we are, but that he never did any wrong.

Jesus the Man

Christians believe Jesus experienced a real human life, knowing human emotions, but he was different in that he never did any wrong. Christians believe they can pray to Jesus knowing he understands what life is like.

Group activity

- Choose one person in each group as the "sculptor".

- Ask the sculptor to arrange the rest of the group in such a way as to express the feelings listed below. The group must co–operate. They are the "clay" the sculptor works on.

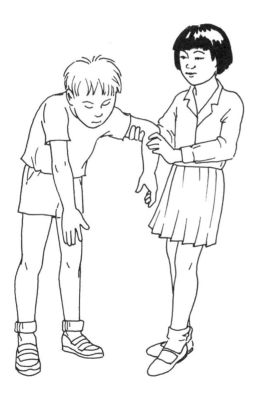

Anger: "Jesus and the Moneychangers", page 34.
Sadness: "Jesus is Arrested", page 48.
Acceptance: "Jesus the King", page 33.
Exhaustion: "Calming the Storm", Book 2, page 92.
Love: "Welcoming the Children", Book 1, page 35.
Relaxed: at Martha and Mary's home, Book 1, page 10.

Christians believe Jesus was "one of us", he experienced human life. He knew friendship and betrayal, joy and sorrow, laughter and pain. Because he knows what human life is like, Christians believe they can pray knowing he understands.

Welcome

Read the Story "Jesus the King" on page 33.

When Jesus entered Jerusalem he was given a royal welcome. People laid their coats down and made a carpet of palm leaves.

Activity

- Read the poem below. What do you think it is about?

- Underline any difficult words and find out what they mean.

The Donkey

G.K. Chesterton

When fishes flew and forests walked
And figs grew upon thorn,
Some moment when the moon was blood
Then surely I was born.

With monstrous head and sickening cry
And ears like errant wings
The devil's walking parody
On all four–footed things.

The tattered outlaw of the earth,
Of ancient crooked will;
Starve, scourge, deride me: I am dumb,
I keep my secret still.

Fools ! For I also had my hour;
One far fierce hour and sweet:
There was a shout about my ears,
And palms before my feet.

From *The Lion Book
of Christian Poetry*

- The poet sometimes uses words which start with the same sound, this is called alliteration. For example "four footed", "ears like errant wings". Can you find other examples of alliteration?

- Where does the rhyme come?

- How many beats of syllables are there in each line? Do the beats form a pattern?

I Am

Read the passage called "I Am Sayings" on page 35.

Activity

- Draw the outline of a person and write "I Am" above them.

- Inside the figure, paste pictures cut from magazines to represent the different "I Am" sayings of Jesus. Trim them to fit exactly inside the figure.

- Round the outside of the figure, write the different "I Am" sayings.

- Choose one of the sayings. What do you think it means?

- Find out from Christians what they think it means.

JESUS 2

Understanding the biblical ideas

The last week of Jesus' life is particularly significant for Christians. He entered the city in triumph, welcomed by the crowd on Palm Sunday, only to be condemned by the same people on Good Friday. Jesus' last week was the week before Passover. At this festival, the Jews remembered God rescuing them from Egyptian slavery. The themes of the Passover contain many parallels with the death of Jesus. The lamb was slain by Israelite families in Egypt in lieu of the death of the first–born (Book 2, pages 49 and 81): the New Testament refers to Jesus as a "lamb" slain. Passover is about freedom, the death of Jesus is about freedom from the slavery of sin and the defeat of evil. The Last Supper was probably a Passover meal shared by Jesus with his disciples, although there is some debate about this. It certainly has all the significance of a Passover meal.

The Jewish trial of Jesus was irregular, though the charge of blasphemy would probably have been upheld in a full court. Jesus' claims were either true or blasphemous. Jesus was retried before the Romans. At this point the charge was changed to a political one, the subtleties of Jewish religious law being outside the scope of the Romans. Pilate declared Jesus innocent but was afraid to let him go. Palestine was a hotbed of unrest and if he let go someone acclaimed as a "Messiah" he might have risked a revolt.

Jesus was buried quickly because of the Sabbath, which began on Friday evening. The normal preparations were done in a hurry, so the women waited until Sunday morning to do the final act of service for Jesus, placing scented herbs on his body. Christians talk of three days in the tomb. Jewish days are counted inclusively (part of a day counts as a day). They are also counted evening to evening — a day commencing at sunset.

After three days Jesus rose again. He met his disciples periodically over forty days. The ascension was when Jesus said *"au revoir"*. He disappeared in a cloud. A cloud is the symbol of the presence of God. His going away initiated the coming of the Holy Spirit in a new way. The Holy Spirit is the replacement for the earthly presence of Jesus: he is able to be present with every believer in a way that Jesus on earth could not be.

Introducing the passages

Discuss special meals with the children, and foods which have a significance. Look at the story of the Last Supper.

Explore in drama the idea of being arrested (not Jesus' arrest).

Read the story of Jesus' arrest.

Talk about sad times and happy times, and the contrast they cause in our feelings. Contrast the story of Jesus' death with his resurrection.

Discuss the difference between *au revoir* and goodbye. When Jesus said goodbye to his friends, it was more like *au revoir*. It was: "See you again." Read the story of the ascension.

Other useful passages

The section entitled "Jesus 1", pages 31–35.

The section entitled "Special Stories of Jesus", pages 18–22.

Other stories told by Jesus can be found on pages 7, 63, 67; Book 1, pages 63, 78, 79–80, 95, 99.

Miracles performed by Jesus can be found in Book 1, pages 6, 7, 8; pages 32, 36.

Other events in the life of Jesus can be found on pages 8, 95; Book 1, pages 7, 10, 22, 35, 51–52, 81; Book 2, pages 34, 63, 105, 106, 107.

Teaching of Jesus can be found on pages 62, 97; Book 1, pages 36, 37, 68–69, 83; Book 2, pages 19, 20, 22.

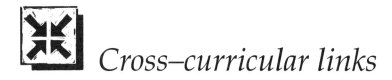

Cross–curricular links

English
- Research recipes for special Easter food and the meaning behind them. (2)
- Make a round–the–world Easter booklet, containing recipes, customs, and celebrations from many different countries and traditions. Some useful books:
  The Lion Easter Book by M Batchelor (Lion, 1987)
  Soul Cakes and Shish Kebabs by A Paraiso and J Mayled (RMEP, 1987).
  Feasting for Festivals by J Wilson (Lion, 1990).
  Pancakes and Painted Eggs by J Chapman (Hodder and Stoughton, 1981). This is out of print but available from libraries. (3)
- Try advertising your booklet, and selling it at a profit for a charity. (3)

Mathematics
- Look at Escher's designs and make your own tessellations for crosses, and other symbols of Christianity. Begin with an oblong and cut, then rearrange and stick. Draw around them and colour appropriately. (4)
- Using recipes researched in English, bake bread and cakes for Easter. This will involve costing, weighing and measuring. (1, 2)

Music
- What kind of music would suit the words of the last days of Jesus' life from the jubilant entry into Jerusalem until his crucifixion? Try and make music which is appropriate. Listen to some sad music, e.g. Verdi's "Requiem", parts of Stainer's "Crucifixion", and parts of Mauder's "Olivet to Calvary". (1, 2)

Art
- Look at classic paintings depicting scenes from the trial and crucifixion (choose sensitively). What colours are used? Which colours depict happiness, sadness, darkness, and lightness of mood? Compare these with modern pictures of the crucifixion, e.g. Salvador Dali. (2)
- Look at icons of Jesus. What message about Jesus is the icon communicating? (2)
- Design and produce a cross using a variety of stitches on canvas or card. Look at the various designs of crosses. (1) (TAT 1, 2)

PE/Dance
- Explore the theme of Easter in movement and dance — from sadness to joy. Still, slow, heavy movements for sadness. Light, fast movements for joy. (KS 1/2)
- In pairs use body sculpture to "sculpt" one person into a sad pose. In eight small moves can the sculptor change it into a joyful pose? (KS 2)

Geography
- Use maps to locate the places mentioned in the stories. Look at the extent of the Roman Empire at that time — which countries did it control? (1)
- Look at the travel brochure for the Holy Land. Can you find any of the places named in the New Testament? Find out how the daily life in Israel/Judah was, and still is, affected by its landscape, position, and weather. (1, 2, 3, 4)

History
- Discuss significance of BC/AD for Christians. (1)
- Look at the extent of the Roman Empire including Britain. Jesus' death was affected by Roman Law — find out about this and about Roman courts. (1, 2, 3)

THE LAST SUPPER
Matthew 26.17–35; Mark 14.12–26 ▶ *page 47*

A Christian perspective
This story brings out Jesus' awareness that he is going to die and he links his death to the Passover. This may not have been a proper Passover meal: the dating is difficult, but the meal does have many Passover elements. Just as the lamb was slain instead of the first–born, so Christians believe Jesus died for the sake of humanity.

Points of interest
1. There are four cups of wine at a Passover. A blessing was normally said over them. One such blessing is: "Blessed be thou, Lord our God, King of the world, who hast created the fruit of the vine." The bread was similarly blessed: "Blessed be thou, Lord our God, King of the world, who brings forth bread from the earth."
2. The "cock crow" was between 12 am and 3 am. This watch was known as cock crow by the Romans. There were also plenty of cockerels in Jerusalem that could have crowed.

JESUS IS ARRESTED
Matthew 26.36–56, 58 ▶ *page 48*

A Christian perspective
The main point of this story for Christians is that Jesus went willingly to the cross because he knew there was no other way. He did not relish it: he dreaded the pain and the separation from God. Christians believe that Jesus carried the sins of the world when he was on the cross and that this separated him from his father. This is a difficult idea to explain to young children. For young children it is sufficient to say that he died a painful and lonely death out of love for others.

Points of interest
1. Jesus describes the coming events as a "cup of suffering". In the Bible, life is often described as a cup. It can be full of happiness, suffering, or other qualities.
2. Judas was paid thirty pieces of silver for Jesus — the price of a male slave. Joseph in the Old Testament cost twenty. Thirty pieces of silver was looked upon as a paltry sum, which shows how little was thought of Jesus.
3. Jesus may have prayed regularly in Gethsemane, in which case Judas would have known where to find him. Judas uses the kiss of greeting to identify Jesus.

JESUS DIES
Matthew 27.45–66; Luke 22.63–65; 23.38–56; Mark 15.16–47; John 19.25–30 ▶ *page 49*

A Christian perspective
The crucifixion is a difficult story to handle in the classroom. The main point for Christians is who was dying and why, not the details of how he died. Dwelling on the torture involved can be very upsetting for some children. It is also advisable to avoid direct drama on the passion as this can be traumatic. Christians believe that Jesus stayed on the cross because he had a job to do. It was love that held him there, not the nails. In some way, Jesus died for the sins of the world. The cross was a battlefield. He took on hatred, sin, death, and injustice, and showed that love could triumph over them all.

Points of interest
1. Crucifixion was the death of slaves, thieves and rebels. Death could sometimes take several days. Jesus died in only six hours. He was offered wine mixed with myrrh, an opiate, but he refused it.
2. Jesus was tried by the Jewish court, the

Sanhedrin, but sentenced to death by a Roman one. The Romans may not have allowed the Jews to impose the death penalty at the time.
3. Criminals were usually buried in a public field outside the city. Jesus was buried quickly because Jewish Law did not allow bodies to remain unburied on the Sabbath, and so they had to be buried before the Sabbath started on the Friday evening.
4. The Roman soldiers' words can be translated "a son of God". Luke reports the soldier's words as "Truly this was a righteous man".
5. Jesus was the eldest son. His mother, a widow, would have been his responsibility.

MARY MEETS JESUS AGAIN
Matthew 28.1–10; John 20.1–18 ▶ *page 51*

A Christian perspective
This story centres on the complete surprise of the resurrection. No one is expecting it: even when Mary meets Jesus, she does not recognize him because she assumes he is dead.

Points of interest
1. Just as the news of Jesus' birth was given to shepherds, a group of outcasts whose testimony was not recognized in court, so the news of the resurrection was given to a woman whose status was low in society and whose testimony was also invalid in court.
2. Rock tombs were the privilege of the wealthy. Jesus was given his tomb by Joseph of Arimathea.
3. Mary recognizes Jesus only when she hears his voice. She had spent a long time listening to him as a teacher.

JESUS SAYS GOODBYE
Acts 1.1–11 ▶ *page 52*

A Christian perspective
The main point of the ascension for Christians is that it is *au revoir,* not goodbye. Jesus goes away but assures them that he will return. This can be understood in two ways: Jesus' place is taken by the Holy Spirit who becomes the disciples' invisible companion; Jesus will come again at the end of time.

Points of interest
1. Jesus disappears in a cloud. A cloud often represents God's presence or glory. A "cloud"

led the Israelites through the wilderness and covered Mount Sinai when the Law was given to Moses.

2. There are two men present in white clothing. These are described as angels. Angels do not always wear white and they don't usually have wings. Normally they are seen as good "strangers" with messages from God. The word "angel" means "messenger". The two angels act as witnesses. Two witnesses are the minimum requirement in a Jewish court.

3. People often worry about ideas such as "up" and "down" in relation to the ascension and try to avoid such language. "Up" is generally used of heaven because anywhere beyond the earth appears to be "up" and it is difficult to communicate the idea of leaving earth in non–spatial terms.

The Last Supper

Matthew 26.17–35; Mark 14.12–26

Jesus looked at his disciples, gathered around the table with him. He had so much to tell them, and he knew time was running out. He knew how frightened they would be very soon, and he knew that much of what he had to say would upset them. But later, when all these things were over, they would understand what he had been saying. He thought how indignant they were just now, when he had insisted that one of them was about to betray him to his enemies. They hadn't wanted to believe that! Now, they just looked very confused.

He had begun the Passover meal in the usual way, but then, after thanking God for the bread which he broke into pieces for them, he had added new words — new words explaining the new meal he was introducing to them tonight. "The bread is my body broken for you," he had said. "In the future, when you gather together to eat bread like this, remember that my body was given into death for you!"

Now at the end of the meal, he lifted the wine. "This wine is a sign of the new agreement, sealed in my blood," he told them. "You are to remember, as you drink it in the future, that my blood was given for you and for many others, to win forgiveness for you."

The disciples were even more confused. Did Jesus mean he was going to die? They had suspected that he meant that on other occasions too, but why should he die? And how?

Jesus knew how puzzled they were. Soon, he thought, you will know some of the answers. He remembered that he still had to warn them. "Tonight, you will all run away from me," he told them, "because you will be terrified by what happens. But I will go back to Galilee ahead of you, and I will see you there. Remember that."

Peter was angry and hurt. "I will never abandon you, Jesus, even if it means I have to die with you."

Jesus smiled at him sadly. "Peter," he said quietly, "you will deny that you even know me before the night is past — before the cock crows." But Peter did not believe him.

Together, the disciples and Jesus sang their Passover hymns. Then Jesus led them out of the borrowed room, and over to a quiet garden, in which he could speak to his Father alone.

Jesus is Arrested

Matthew 26.36–56; 58

In the quiet shelter of the olive trees in Gethsemane, Jesus was praying. This was an agonizing time for him. He knew what was to come — the cruel, painful death, and, even worse, the separation from his loving Father, God. "Father," he prayed, "if you can do this in any other way, then please take this cup of suffering away from me. But, whatever it costs me, I want to do only what you wish me to do. I only want to obey you."

Jesus had left his three closest friends — Peter, James, and John — to pray together in another part of the garden. But they were tired. Three times Jesus returned to them, and each time they were sleeping.

How lonely and frightened Jesus felt! That third time, he asked sadly, "Couldn't you stay awake with me just for a little while? But it's too late now. They are already coming to arrest me. Look!"

To their horror, the disciples saw a group of armed men coming — Judas was leading them. The other disciples rushed to join Jesus. Judas came straight up to Jesus and kissed him in greeting. This was the signal Judas had promised: men rushed forward and arrested Jesus.

The disciples were horrified. Some of them were prepared to fight to save him, but Jesus stopped them. "There is no need to defend me," he said, "and you men need not have come armed to arrest me. I have to do this. I won't resist or try to escape."

Then the disciples panicked: what would happen to them now? They ran away — all of them, except Peter. He hid among the trees, and then followed secretly while Jesus was dragged to his trial.

Jesus Dies

Matthew 27.45–66; Luke 22.63–65; 23.38–56; Mark 15.16–47;

John 19.25–30

So they crucified Jesus. The High Priest and the Sanhedrin had tried him and found him guilty, because he said he was the Son of God. He'd then been dragged in front of Pilate, the Roman Governor. Pilate believed Jesus to be innocent, but when he told the crowd that he could release him, they chose a murderer to be released instead. Pilate soon realized that there would be a riot in Jerusalem if he did not let Jesus' enemies have their own way. So Jesus was flogged, and suffered cruel mockery from the soldiers. On the board above his cross, on which his crime should have been written, they wrote: "Jesus, King of the Jews." And they crucified him.

But even as he hung there dying, Jesus was thinking of other people and of his special mission from God. He asked his Father to forgive the very people who were killing him. Two thieves were also suffering crucifixion with him. One of them asked Jesus to forgive him for all he had done wrong. Jesus told him that he did forgive him, and that the man was now one of God's friends.

Then Jesus thought about Mary, his mother, who had looked after him as a child. She was there, watching, almost unable to bear the sight, but determined to stay with her son until he died. Jesus saw John, the disciple he especially loved, and shouted down to him, "Look at Mary, John! Look after her as if she was your own mother."

Feeling completely alone, Jesus cried out in despair, "My God, why have you abandoned me?" But then, as he felt that he could not live for much longer, Jesus shouted in triumph: "It is finished!" He had completed what he had to do to save his friends. Finally, he prayed again to God. "Father, I put myself in your hands." And he died.

Immediately the earth shook so that the rocks crumbled. In the Temple, the great heavy curtain, hung to separate the Holy Place from the ordinary people, was torn in half — from the top to the bottom.

When the Roman officer saw how Jesus died, he exclaimed, "Surely this man must have been the Son of God!"

But some of the watchers were aware only of their own sorrow and feeling of loss. They were worried, too, about Jesus' burial. Where could they bury him? They were short of time, too, for it would soon be the Sabbath.

Someone else had thought of all this, too, and had already made his plans. Joseph of Arimathea went to Pilate and asked his permission to bury Jesus' body. Joseph was an important Jewish leader. He had been a follower of Jesus for a while, but had kept this a secret because he was frightened of his fellow leaders. Now, though, he had decided it was time to stop hiding.

So Joseph, followed by some of the women who had travelled with Jesus, took the body. They wrapped it in clean linen, and then laid it on the slab cut into the wall of the tomb which Joseph had prepared for his own burial. They rolled the great stone over the entrance. Then, sorrowfully, they left the body for a while, for it was the Sabbath.

Jesus Dies — continued

But the chief priests and the Pharisees were still not satisfied. This Jesus had proved too clever for them before. They were not going to give his followers a chance to trick them now. They went to Pilate, asking for a guard on the tomb: "For remember, Jesus said that he would rise again. What would happen if the disciples stole the body in order to pretend he was alive again? Then we would have trouble in the city!"

So a guard was posted at the tomb, and they set a seal over the stone. "No one will get in — or out of there now!" they said gloatingly.

Mary Meets Jesus Again

Matthew 28.1–10; John 20.1–18

As soon as they could after the Sabbath, very early in the morning, Mary Magdalene and some of the other women hurried to the tomb. They brought with them expensive and precious spices and ointments to anoint Jesus, for there had been no time to prepare the body properly when he was buried. As they approached the tomb, they were astonished to see that the great stone had been rolled away. Their first thought was that Jesus' enemies had taken his body for some reason. They rushed up to the tomb — and stopped in amazement.

There, they could see two angels sitting on the slab on which the body had lain. The women were terrified and bewildered. One of the angels said, "Don't be frightened. You are looking for Jesus in the wrong place. He's alive again — just as he told you he would be. So don't look for him here in a tomb. Go and tell the disciples that he will meet them in Galilee, as he promised."

The women hurried back to the house where the disciples were hiding — they were all afraid that Jesus' enemies might arrest them next. The women told them all they had heard and seen, and Peter and John rushed out to the tomb. They weren't sure whether the women were right about Jesus, but obviously something had happened to the body. Mary Magdelene, confused but desperately wanting to believe the angels, followed the men. Once John had seen the tomb himself, with the linen cloths lying on the slab, he believed that Jesus was indeed alive. He and Peter hurried back to report this to the other disciples.

But Mary stayed near the tomb. She was crying. She was confused: could it be true that Jesus was alive? If only she could really believe it! But what if someone had stolen the body? She realized that someone had joined her. She turned to him, thinking it was the gardener. Perhaps he could help her. She wiped her eyes roughly. "Sir," she begged, "if you know where his body is, please tell me."

Then the man said, "Mary." And Mary recognized his voice. It was Jesus! It was true — he was alive!

"Tell my disciples that I will soon return to my Father," he told her.

So once again, Mary hurried back to the disciples. But this time she could say, "I have seen Jesus! He is alive!"

Jesus Says Goodbye

Acts 1.1–11

Jesus spent time with his disciples after he had risen from death. But they knew he would not stay for ever. He had told them that he must return to his Father. One day Jesus walked with his friends out into the countryside. There, he turned to them, and said, "You must now go all over the world to tell people about me, explaining to them how they can become friends with God. Wait in Jerusalem for the Holy Spirit whom the Father will send. He will give you the power you need to teach and heal people."

Then, while they were watching him, he was taken up, into heaven. A cloud hid him, and they could see him no more. And suddenly two men in white were standing by the disciples. "Why are you standing there looking upwards? Your friend Jesus, who today has left you, will one day return."

The disciples returned to Jerusalem, comforting each other by recalling Jesus' promises about their future. They knew that they must start this great mission which Jesus had given them. But first they must wait for God to send his Holy Spirit to live in them, to help them as they worked.

Servant Master

Read the story of "The Last Supper" on page 47 and John 13.1–20.

Activity

- What words come to your mind when you think of the word "servant".

- Now write down the words that come to mind when you hear the word "master".

- Choose a partner. One person should be the master and one the servant. The master should give the servant an order such as, "Answer the door!" The servant should then mime carrying out the order, but before the servant has finished, the master should issue another order. Keep this up for one minute — but the master must make so many demands that the servant never has time to complete anything. Swap places and repeat the exercise.

- Choose a new partner. This time, the master gives orders but the servant can ask for help to carry them out. The master must not refuse. Can the servant get the master to do the work?

Think about it

Christians call Jesus both Lord (master) and servant. Read the story of the washing of the disciples' feet. How did he act as servant? This act was only one way in which Jesus was a servant. He said that he came to serve humanity. How do you think he did that?

The Sun

Read the story called "Mary Meets Jesus Again" on page 51.

A sun is sometimes used as a symbol of Jesus. It is also a symbol of the resurrection, for it sets and rises just as the Bible says Jesus died and rose again.

Activity

- Take a plain paper plate and cut out a small circle the size of a ten pence piece in the centre. Cut an odd number of notches around the edge.

- Decide whether you are making a rising sun, a setting sun, or a sun at its height, this will decide what colours you will use. When you have decided which type of sun you want to make, choose the colour wools you will need.

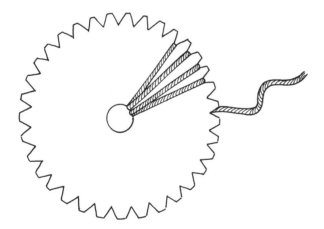

- Sellotape the end of a piece of wool to the back of the plate and wind your wool around the plate, taking the wool through the centre hole each time and over the notches. When your circle is complete, sellotape the end of the wool to the back.

- This is the basis for your sun. Weave different materials of a suitable colour round your circle to create a sun.

The Key to the Kingdom

Choose any story from this section for this activity.

The "Key to the Kingdom" is a traditional poem. It is like a Russian doll, one thing inside another.

This is the key of the kingdom.
In that kingdom there is a city.
In that city there is a town.
In that town there is a street.
In that street there is a lane.
In that lane there is a yard.
In that yard there is a house.
In that house there is a room.
In that room there is a bed.
On that bed there is a basket.
In that basket there are some flowers.
Flowers in the basket, basket in the bed,
bed in the room, &c. &c.

(Traditional, from *The Nursery Rhyme Book,* Omega)

Activity

- Write your own "Key to the Kingdom" poem.

  Always start your poem with the line: "This is the key to the kingdom."

- Read your story carefully, and select the moment in your story with which you want to end your poem.

- Example: story — "Mary meets Jesus Again", page 51.

  For this example you would have to go from the kingdom, to the city, to the garden, to the tomb.

- Add adjectives, describing words, to make your poem more interesting. Don't just write "city", describe the city: "busy city", "cool garden", etc.

Example: This is the key to the kingdom.
In that kingdom lies a great city.
In that city stands a cool garden.
In that garden is a cold tomb.
Outside the tomb weeps a lone woman,
Grieving for her friend.

• Finish your poem with a drawing of a key.

The Cross Symbol

Christians use the symbol of a cross to remember the death and resurrection of Jesus. They use a cross with Jesus on it to remember his death (a crucifix). They use an empty cross to remember his resurrection.

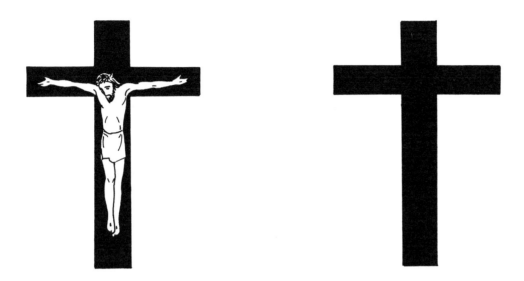

To Christians today, the cross is a symbol of God's love. To Roman Christians, the cross was a symbol of cruel torture. Roman Christians often used the anchor cross, which reminded them that God would hold them firm in times of trouble and persecution, as an anchor holds a ship firm in a storm.

Think about it

Can you think of another reason why they might have chosen an anchor? Discuss this with some friends.

PRAYER

Understanding the biblical ideas

Prayer is about a relationship with God: it is a way of life for a Christian, not just an event that happens at certain times. There are many different types of prayer:

- Praise prayers: these tell God how great he is. Mary's Song is a praise prayer.
- Thank you prayers: these thank God for what he has done. Psalm 136 is a thank you prayer.
- Sorry prayers: sorry prayers ask for forgiveness. Psalm 51 is a sorry prayer.
- Intercessions: these are asking prayers. Asking is only a small part of prayer. People can ask for things for themselves or others but these prayers are not a shopping list. Christians expect God to say no to things that will be harmful or wrong.
- Help prayers: these are often said in times of stress or trouble. Psalm 69 is a help prayer.

The Book of Psalms contains many prayers. Most of them are praise prayers and would have been sung or spoken out loud during worship. We have, preserved in the Bible, the prayers of people such as Moses and Abraham, David and Solomon. For all of these people, prayer was an important part of life. Jeremiah spoke very plainly to God when he was upset. Daniel prayed three times a day. Prayer was an important part of Jesus' life: he often got up early to pray. He prayed before he chose his disciples. He prayed in the Garden of Gethsemane, and he prayed on the cross.

Prayer is not twisting God's arm to do what we want him to do. God is not reluctant to help as the friend in the parable of "The Friend at Midnight" is. Neither does he have to be forced to help as the unjust judge is in that parable.

Prayer does not have to be in any particular language or style: what matters is the heart of the person praying, as the parable of "The Pharisee and the Tax Collector" makes clear. In the Lord's Prayer, Jesus gives an example of how to pray. This prayer includes asking for bodily needs to be met (bread). Prayer can be very practical.

Introducing the passages

Discuss with the children the different ways we communicate. Talk about the role of communication within a relationship. Prayer is like the conversation that takes place within any committed relationship.

The idea of fan clubs can be used to introduce praise prayers which can lead into Mary's prayer. Thank you letters and cards can be used to introduce Psalm 136.

SOS and Mayday messages can be used to explore help prayers such as Psalm 69. Psalm 51 is not included here, but short sections of it can then be paraphrased from the Bible.

Use a set of Russian dolls to explore the idea of God looking on the heart during prayer, rather than just listening to the words. Follow this by reading the story of "The Pharisee and the Tax Collector". Talk about being on different sides. The stories of "The Unjust Judge", and "The Friend at Midnight" are about God being on humanity's side: he does not have to be persuaded to help.

Other useful passages

"Daniel and the Lions", page 107.

"Daniel and the King's Dreams", Book 2, page 8.

"Jesus is Tempted", page 32, "Jesus is Arrested", page 48.

"Elijah and the Prophets of Baal", Book 2, page 79.

"Elisha and the Syrians", Book 2, page 91.

"Hannah's Precious Gift", Book, page 104.

"Psalm 139", Book 1, page 34.

"Psalm 23", page 81.

"Paul meets Jesus", Book 2, page 64.

"Jesus and his Friends", Book 1, page 7.

Cross–curricular links

English

- Look at Dürer's painting "The Praying Hands" — why do we keep our hands still to pray? (1)
- Discuss rosary beads. How do they help people concentrate in prayer? (1)
- Look at the section of *Presenting Poetry* by S Palmer and P Mc Call (Oliver and Boyd) called "Hands together, eyes closed". Write your own prayer–poem. Look at some of the Bible' s prayer–poems, you will find these in the book of Psalms. The book *Praise* by A J McCallen (Collins) has many or these prayer–poems rephrased for children. Read the poem "Vespers" by A A Milne (*The Oxford Book of Children' s Verse*). Make up your own poem about a child saying their prayers. (3)
- Write a coat hanger poem about prayer. Write the word "Prayer" down the middle of the page. The first line should have a P in it, preferably near the middle. The second line should have an R in it (see Book 2, page 98 for details). (3)
- Create a sketch based on a fan meeting their idol. Explore the idea of praise as "fan mail to God". (1)
- Dramatize the stories of "The Friend at Midnight" and "The Unjust Judge". (1)

Music

- Many hymns are like prayers set to music, as are the psalms. Interview a number of people about their favourite hymns and why they like them. Is it the words or music they particularly like? Write up the results of your interviews and make them into a book, including the hymn and a photograph of the person as part of the write–up. Record the chosen hymns on a cassette to accompany your class book of favourite hymns. These can be used as the basis for a series of assemblies. (2) (EAT 1, 2)
- If your school uses the Lord's Prayer, try singing it instead of saying it. (1)
- Mary's prayer (the Magnificat, page 64) is often sung. The hymn "Tell out my soul" is a sung version of it. Children can listen to different ways the prayer has been expressed in music. Schubert, Vivaldi, Bach, Cavalli, Palestrina, and Tippett have all produced musical settings for it. What type of music would Indian Christians use for the Magnificat? Explore the way various musical traditions could be used. (2)

Geography

- Collect prayers from around the world and display them round a large map indicating where they come from, or map them using the index/contents page of an atlas giving coordinates (six figures) for each one. The following books may be useful: *The Lion Book of Children's Prayers* (Lion), and *Another Day: Prayers of the Human Family* by J Carden (Triangle). (1)
- Find various places where people go on pilgrimage (Iona, Walsingham, etc.) Plan a journey from your house to that place using public transport. Use a timetable to do this and cost the journey. (1)
- Explore places of pilgrimage in other countries and plan journeys with their routes and costings. (1) (MAT 1, 2)

Art

- Draw hands at prayer. Look at the picture of praying hands by Dürer for inspiration. Use pastels for this, or charcoal, or coloured pencils you can dip in water. (1, 2)
- Express the story of "The Friend at Midnight" as a cartoon. (1)
- Read the extract from Psalm 69. Choose one of the images from this psalm to paint as a picture. (1)

History

- Look at places of pilgrimage in different periods of history. (1)
- Explore the story behind some of the centres of pilgrimage: e.g. Canterbury (Thomas à Becket). (1)
- Look at famous prayers from different periods of history and how they reflect the events and thinking of the time. Prayers from all periods of history can be found in the book *The Lion Book of Famous Prayers*. (1)

PE/Dance

- Look at the different types of prayer: praise, sorry, thank you, please, and help. Prayers can be danced as well as spoken. What would a sorry dance look like? What would a praise dance look like? Use a piece of flowing fabric in your dance to help capture different types of movement. (KS 1/2)

JESUS' ADVICE ON PRAYER
Matthew 6.5–15; 7.7–11 ▶ *page 62*

A Christian perspective

The Bible stresses that prayer is about a relationship. It is not just asking for things. Some

Pharisees behaved as if the most important thing about prayer was the form of the words and the audience who heard it. People did not usually pray on street corners, but they could make sure they were in a public place when it was time for the afternoon prayers.

Points of interest

The Lord's Prayer:

1. The word Jesus sometimes used for father is "Abba" — "Daddy"— which is the familiar form for father in Aramaic. It also denoted obedience and respect.
2. "In heaven" — this is a reverential way of referring to God.
3. God's name stood for God himself so "May your holy name be honoured" means, "May you be honoured in the world".
4. "Bread" could just be ordinary daily "bread". This is included because God is concerned about human welfare. Bread in this case represents all food.
5. "Debt" is the underlying Aramaic word for sin, here translated as "wrong" (trespass in the older English versions). The word trespass is literally a false step, "putting a foot wrong".
6. "The hard testing" refers to the trials Christians faced in their daily lives. Christians experienced persecution of varying degrees from the Romans. They were banned from Rome under Claudius, and the persecutions of Nero and Diocletian were savage.

THE PHARISEE AND THE TAX COLLECTOR
Luke 18.9–14 ▶ *page 63*

A Christian perspective

In this parable, Jesus teaches that God notices the "heart" and intention, he does not just listen to the public prayer put on for show. The tax collector had the right requirements for having his prayers listened to: he was sincere and he was only too aware of what he had done wrong. He confirms the Pharisee's opinion of him.

Points of interest

1. The Pharisees were a group of strict Jews. The name means "separated". There were about five or six thousand Pharisees in Jesus' day. Some were like Nicodemus, conscientious and genuine. Others were more concerned about their position in society.
2. The Pharisee prays aloud, standing, as was common. The tax collector, who would have been viewed as a collaborator with the Romans and as a thief, stands apart. He is isolated from the people.

3. One tenth was the minimum offering required by the Law. People were only expected to fast once a year, not twice a week. This Pharisee had done more than the Law required externally, but his attitude to God and to others was wrong.

MARY'S PRAYER
Luke 1.46–55 ▶ *page 64*

A Christian perspective

Mary's song of praise is very like Hannah's song on the birth of Samuel. A thousand years separated the two women but their thoughts are the same.

In the Bible, God is often shown as using people whom society looks upon as being unimportant. Mary was a young, unmarried girl — three qualifications that would have reduced her status in a society which valued men, age, and the ability to have children. Hannah and Elizabeth similarly were low in status because they had no children.

Points of interest

1. Children were seen as a blessing from God: conversely, if a woman had no children, people thought God was not pleased with her. A woman's status went up on the birth of a child. She became known as "Mother of..."
2. This song is known as "The Magnificat" from the opening Latin word of the song in the earlier translations of the Bible: "My soul doth magnify the Lord". The song celebrates God's care, goodness and his values, which are often different from the world's. He honours the poor and the powerless. The Bible is crammed with examples of this. Joseph went from being a prisoner to Prime Minister; Moses from being a wanted man and shepherd to leader; David from being a shepherd to king; Jesus was a carpenter. Christians describe God as a God of the unexpected, who sees the value of women, children and the poor, even if others don't.

A HELP PRAYER AND A THANK YOU PRAYER
Psalm 69 ▶ *page 65, Psalm 136* ▶ *page 66*

A Christian perspective

Psalm 69 is a cry of distress to a God who is seen as the rescuer, the saviour, the one who fights for the people. Troubles are likened to a sea that threatens to engulf the victim. They are also likened to quicksand and a deep pit that is like the mouth of an animal.

Psalm 136 describes God as the author of all things, therefore gratitude is due to him. In this psalm he is referred to as creator, rescuer, and provider. People rightly point out that not everyone has food — some starve. Does this mean God has failed? The Bible is realistic about famine. It was a common experience. The Bible asserts that God made the world fertile. This world produces enough food to feed itself and still have food left over. The Middle East has fertile areas and drought–stricken areas. The problem is not a problem of fertility however, it is a problem of sharing and distribution.

Points of interest

1. The victim in Psalm 69 must have been in serious trouble if his family rejected him.
2. Lord of Lords and God of Gods. This is a Hebrew way of using a superlative. It means the "God above all gods". Jesus was known as "King of Kings".
3. Psalm 136 may have been read antiphonally: one person would have said the lines and a group would have chanted the response.

THE UNJUST JUDGE AND THE FRIEND AT MIDNIGHT

Luke 18.1–8; 11.5–13; ▶ *page 67*

A Christian perspective
The point of both of these parables is that God wants to answer prayer. Christians believe he does not have to be nagged into doing it. Answers come in three forms: "Yes", "No", and "Wait".

Points of interest

1. The Law was very plain about fairness. This judge may have taken a bribe to ignore the widow's case, which was against the law. Corruption was seen as an insult to God, as it did not reflect his character (truth), and because it hurt his people.
2. A widow was in a very serious position economically, particularly, as seems to be the case here, if she did not have a son.
3. In the parable of "The Friend at Midnight", it must be remembered that hospitality was very important. This is what makes the friend so insistent. Journeys were sometimes undertaken at night to avoid the heat of the day.
4. The family all slept together on a raised platform in the house. One person getting up would have disturbed the whole family.
5. Bread was the staple diet of the poor. It was cooked daily. Three loaves was more than enough for one person.

Jesus' Advice on Prayer

Matthew 6.5–15; 7.7–11

Pray in Secret

Some people love to pray in public, so that other people will see them. They want others to think that they are really good. They stand in the synagogues, or even on the corners of the street! But you should pray in private, in your own room — with the door closed — so that no other person can see you. God sees everything: he will know that you are praying, and he is the only one who needs to know. Remember, too, that God is not impressed by very long prayers. Some people think that if they pray for a long time, God is more likely to hear and answer them. God knows what you need, even before you ask him for it. So you don't need to talk on and on about it.

God Wants to Answer

Ask God for all that you need. If your children asked you for some bread, would you be so cruel as to give them a stone? Or a snake instead of a fish? No, of course you wouldn't, because you love them — and you are just ordinary people. Just think, then, how many more good things your perfect Father — God — will be happy to give you, his child.

The Lord's Prayer

Jesus told his followers. "This is the sort of prayer that will please God.

"Our Father in Heaven.
May your holy name be honoured.
May your Kingdom come, and
May your will be done on earth
As it is done in heaven.
Give us today our daily bread,
And forgive us the wrong we do
As we forgive others.
May we not face the hard testing
But save us from the power of evil.
For to you belongs the Kingdom
The power
And the glory,
For ever,
Amen."

The Pharisee and the Tax Collector

Luke 18.9–14

Jesus looked around at the people listening to his teaching. He knew that some of them were thinking that they need not do as he said. "I'm alright," they thought. "I haven't done anything wrong — not like all these other people." So Jesus told a story to show these people that they were mistaken.

"One day, two men arrived in the Temple Courts at the same time. They both came to pray to God. One of them was a Pharisee, a man who studied God's Law. He looked around him before he began to pray. He hoped that other people would notice how devoted to God he seemed. He caught sight of the other man. 'He's in the right place, anyway!' he thought nastily. 'He certainly needs to pray!' For the other man was a tax collector.

"The Pharisee stood up straight, lifted up his arms and began to pray. 'God, I am glad that I am not wicked, like so many other people are — such as this tax collector! I always do the right things. I go without food twice a week — twice! And I always bring a whole tenth of my income as an offering to God.'

"But the tax collector stayed at the back of the Court. He wouldn't even look up, he was so ashamed of himself. He knew he was not perfect. He knew that he did many wrong things, even though he tried hard not to! 'O God,' he prayed, 'please forgive me. Forgive me for the things I have done wrong, and be good to me — even though I do not deserve your love.'

"It was the tax collector whom God forgave," Jesus went on, "because the tax collector knew he had done wrong. God will show he has forgiven anyone who knows they have done wrong and are sorry for their failures. On the other hand, people like that Pharisee, who believe they are perfect and are not sorry for anything, will not be forgiven."

Mary's Prayer

Luke 1.46–55

After the angel had told Mary that she was going to give birth to Jesus, she went to visit her cousin Elizabeth. Elizabeth herself was going to have a son, who would be John the Baptist. While Mary was there, she and Elizabeth talked about what had happened, and about the children they would have. Mary was so full of joy because of all this, that she prayed a beautiful song of praise to God. Here it is.

"I want to shout out how great God is,
Tell everyone what joy he brings!
Even though I am so poor and unimportant,
God has noticed me.
From now on, everyone will know how fortunate I am,
For God has done wonderful things for me.
His care reaches down through the ages,
He has performed great miracles with his power.
He scatters the proud and tumbles kings from their thrones —
But the poor he gently picks up and makes great.
He looks after those who are hungry, filling them with good things to eat. But the rich he sends away empty–handed.
He has always looked after the people of Israel, as he said he would —
And he has kept that promise."

RESOURCE BANK 3: PRAYER

A Help Prayer

Psalm 69

Save me God.
My troubles, like water, reach up to my neck.
I feel as if I am sinking in quicksand.
My sorrow overwhelms me as a flood.
I am hoarse with calling for help,
My eyes are tired with looking for rescue.
My enemies number more than the hairs of my head.
But I have done nothing to deserve this hatred!
You know all about me, God;
You know whether I deserve all this.
My friends and family have turned against me.
They all make fun of me because I believe in you.
But I will continue to pray to you,
Even though I have become a laughing stock!
Please rescue me from all this.
Do not let my sea of troubles overwhelm me:
Don't let this great pit of evil swallow me up,
For I know that you love me.
Answer me quickly.
You know how badly my enemies are treating me.
No one else will help me, or stand up for me.
But you can rescue me.

A Thank You Prayer

Psalm 136

The Lord is good: thank him for everything:
His love goes on for ever.
Thank the God of Gods:
His love goes on for ever.
Thank the Lord of Lords:
His love goes on for ever.
He alone can perform great and wonderful things:
His love goes on for ever.
By his understanding he made the heavens:
His love goes on for ever.
He made the earth and the seas in his wisdom:
His love goes on for ever.
He created the great lights in the sky:
His love goes on for ever.
The sun to rule over the day:
His love goes on for ever.
The moon to rule over the night:
His love goes on for ever.
Give thanks to the God of all the universe.

The Unjust Judge and the Friend at Midnight

Luke 18.1–8; 11.5–13

Jesus spoke about prayer quite often. Sometimes he used stories to show his followers how they should pray, and to teach them about the God who listened to their prayers. Here are two of these.

The Unjust Judge

"There was once a woman who had been treated unfairly by somebody. She kept going to the town's judge, to beg him to sort out the matter for her. Now this judge did not really care about doing his job properly. He did not bother trying to please God by being fair in what he did. He did not care whether people were in trouble or not. But this woman really annoyed him. She wouldn't give up. In the end, he said to himself, 'I'll have to look into this problem for her, because she'll never give me any peace until I do put things right! I really couldn't care less whether she has been cheated or not — but I must stop her coming to me, begging for help!'

"Now," Jesus went on, "if that judge decided to help the woman, just to keep her quiet, how much more will your God help you when you ask him to? Your God loves you and wants to help you. So, keep asking God for what you need, and he will answer you."

The Friend at Midnight

"What would you do if this happened to you? You are in bed at night, with your children settled asleep beside you. Everything is quiet and peaceful. Suddenly there is a loud knocking! Your friend shouts, 'Wake up! Could you please lend me some bread? A friend of mine has just turned up unexpectedly, and I've nothing to give him to eat.' What would you say?

"Perhaps you'd shout back, 'But I'm in bed — and my children are too. I can't get up now!'

"But your friend insists. 'You must lend me some bread. What else can I do?'

"Now, you think, this man is your friend after all, and in any case, if you don't give him some bread, he'll wake up the children. So, up you get, groaning, and take him some bread.

"Remember," Jesus concluded, "God is much more than just a friend. If you keep asking him for something you need, he will give it to you — not grudgingly, like the man in the story — but gladly, because he loves you."

Different Prayers

Activity

Look at the different types of communication below. Choose one type of letter to write and then display it next to a matching prayer. Example: if you choose to write a thank you letter, display it next to a thank you prayer from the Bible or a children's prayer book. If you write a fan letter display it next to a praise prayer, etc.

- Fan Letter: write a fan letter to a favourite personality. Praise prayers are like fan mail to God. Mary's prayer on page 64 is a praise prayer.

- Thanks: write a thank you letter to an imaginary person. Psalm 136, on page 66, is a thank you prayer.

- Sorry: write an imaginary letter of apology for something you have done wrong. Find a sorry prayer in a children's prayer book.

- Asking: write a list of things you would like for yourself or for others. You will find many examples of this kind of prayer in a children's prayer book.

- Help: write an urgent request for help. Psalm 69, on page 65, is a help prayer.

- Just chatting: write an imaginary letter to a friend, telling them pieces of news. Look through a children's prayer book and display your letter next to a prayer that is more like a chat between friends.

Think about it

Prayer is communication with God. It is both talking and listening. Some prayer is silent, some is spoken and some prayers are sung. Prayer is not just for difficult times or when people need help. It is like the everyday communication among members of a family.

The Pharisee and the Tax Collector

Read the story of "The Pharisee and the Tax Collector" on page 63.

Activity

• Look at the picture of the Pharisee and the Tax Collector. Fill in the speech bubbles and the thought clouds.

• What was each person saying? What do you think they were thinking?

Think about it

In the parable of "The Pharisee and the Tax Collector", Jesus surprised people. Everyone would have expected the respectable religious leader to be the one to whom God listened, not a hated tax collector. Tax collectors had a reputation for dishonesty, and they worked for the hated Romans, the enemy. What do you think Jesus was saying in this parable?

Arrow Prayers

An arrow prayer is a short prayer that a person sends to God when they are in the middle of a situation. No one else need know they are praying.

Look at the arrow prayers below.

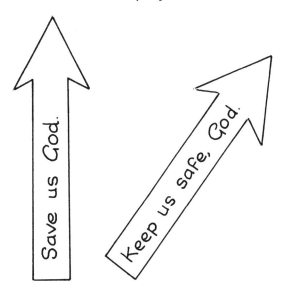

Read one of these stories: Daniel, page 107; Jeremiah, page 108; Paul, page 110.

Write within the arrows the prayer you think they might have prayed.

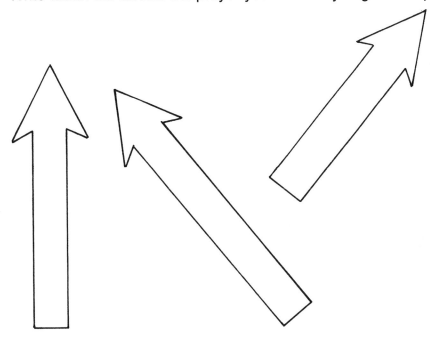

Think about it

Arrow prayers are short and to the point. They can be delivered any time and in any place.

Have there been times when you have prayed a short prayer when no one else would know you were praying? Did you find this helped you?

Candles and Incense

Frankincense was a type of incense given to Jesus. Incense was burnt in worship, and was made of small crystals of sweet–smelling resin which gave off a perfumed smoke. The smoke going upward reminded people that their prayers go to God who is always ready to listen. In some churches, incense and candles are used for the same reason today.

Activity

- Draw the outline of a candle on white paper. Make sure you leave plenty of space above the candle. Draw a wick on your candle.

- Write prayers in long lines to look like smoke coming from the candle.

- Using pastels, colour in the candle itself. How are you going to make the candle look curved?

Think about it

There must be millions of people who pray, yet the Bible says that God listens to each one and longs to answer, but sometimes the answer is "No", or "Wait."

GOD

Understanding the biblical ideas

The concept of God's existence is assumed in the Bible: nowhere do writers set out to prove it. The Bible starts with, "In the beginning God…"

God is not an abstract idea at which people arrive just by thought. God is described as active and involved with humanity. He is a God who shows people what he is like.

God is described in many ways. He is likened, for example, to a shepherd, a rock, a fortress, a judge, a king. Each description brings out different aspects of his nature. Throughout the Bible, God is described as Father. Jesus used the term "Abba", the equivalent of "Daddy", though it also carried the idea of authority. God is described as a mother who cares for her children, and as a devoted husband.

The Bible describes various aspects of the nature of God. God is described as one: he is the God of the whole world and the God of history; there is no other God to rival him. God is also depicted as loving and forgiving, far more ready to forgive than the reluctant Jonah or the elder brother in the parable of the prodigal son. He is seen as just and righteous, and does not let evil go unchecked: God judges what people do, both now and at the end of time. God is powerful and ultimately in charge of the world: the nations are a "drop in the bucket" to him; he is creative, and has created a world of infinite variety.

God is involved with his world. God did not create the world, wind it up and let it go. He is seen in constant interaction with it, providing for the Israelites in the wilderness, leading his people across the desert. Individuals meet God in various situations. Moses meets him in the burning bush, others meet him through an angel or prayer. Some, like Elijah or Paul, hear his "voice". God is not aloof.

The biblical writers use terms such as "the hand of God" or his "eye", but these terms tend to be used metaphorically or poetically.

In the New Testament, the idea of God as Father is developed and Jesus is seen as showing what God is like, in his person and work. The writer John describes God as "love", which is part of his essential nature.

Introducing the passages

Look at things the children have created, or handcrafted objects, and explore the idea of creating.

Discuss the idea of providing for people. Who provides for us and how? Look at the story of God providing. Explore how God provided for the Israelites and how God provides through nature.

Discuss the different titles people have, such as "King", "Duchess", "Princess", etc. What do the titles say about the people? What do God's titles say about him?

Other useful passages

The whole section on "Forgiveness", Book 1, pages 78–83.

The stories in Book 1, pages 37 and 67 illustrate God's care.

The stories on the following show God as judge: pages 5, 6, 18; Book 1, pages 82, 96–97; Book 2, pages 33, 45.

The story in Book 2, page 81, shows God as guide.

For fire as a symbol of God, see the section entitled "Fire", Book 2, pages 77–81.

For God's promises, see the section entitled "Promises", Book 2, pages 45–52.

For God's laws, see the section called "Laws for Living", pages 18–22.

For God communicating see the section headed "Messages", pages 5–8.

The rest of the Moses story can be found in Book 1, pages 19–20, 23; Book 2, pages 21, 49, 77, 81.

The rest of the Elijah story can be found on page 80, Book 1, page 64; Book 2, page 33.

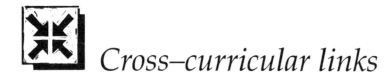

Cross–curricular links

English
- Read the story of *The Magician's Nephew* by C S Lewis (Fontana , Lions) which describes the creation of Narnia. Read *My Secret Life* by M Hebblethwaite (Hunt Thorpe) This is the story of a child's friendship with God. Read *Brown Ears: the adventures of a lost and found rabbit* by S Lawhead (Lion, 1989). This story explores the idea of God's guidance and care in a humorous fashion. (2)
- Look at the book, *Our Two Gardens* by M Hebblethwaite (Hunt Thorpe). Create your own picture book with captions comparing a back garden with the "garden" of the world. (2, 3)
- Poetry — use the format "The Making of…" for poems about the making of various parts of creation: "The making of the spider", "The making of a tree". (3)

Science and Technology
- Create your own mini–environment. What does any mini–environment need to be self–sustaining? What plant container might be best? Think about shape, design, materials. Consider what plants need to grow. Devise a controlled test to show which conditions and factors contribute towards the best mini–environment for plants or mini–beasts. (1, 2) (TAT 1, 2)
- Look closely at the book *Wonderful Earth* by N Butterworth and M Inkpen (Hunt Thorpe). Choose one part of the story of creation. Make one page of a book about that story. Use pop–ups, flaps or slides as the book *Wonderful Earth* does. (4) (TAT 1, 2)

Music
- Listen to the "Hallelujah Chorus" from the *Messiah* and imagine how Handel must have felt when he was writing the music. Listen to parts of *The Creation* by Haydn. (2)
- Using various instruments, can you create sounds to accompany the story of creation. Look at Christian songs such as "The Lord's my Shepherd" to see how Christians express their ideas about God in song. Listen to part of *Elijah* by Mendelssohn. (1)

Personal and Social Education
- How do you feel about things which you have made? Discuss owning things you have made. Discuss the idea of looking after the world, and others, on God's behalf. (EAT 1)

History
- Look at famous characters and see how their beliefs have affected their work. For example: Alfred the Great ("Invaders and Settlers"), Sir Thomas More ("Tudors and Stuarts"), The Cadbury Family ("Victorian Britain"), C S Lewis ("Britain since 1930"). Look at ordinary people and how their beliefs and religious practices affect their daily lives. (1, 2)

PE/Dance
- Explore the creation in dance using music from the music section as a stimulus. (KS 1/2)
- Explore the ideas of wind, fire, and the still quiet voice in movement. (KS 1/2)

GOD THE CREATOR
Genesis 1.1 — 2.4 ▶ *page 79*

A Christian perspective
Christians differ over how this story is interpreted but for all it is important that the world is created by a good God and that creation is deliberate and purposeful, not blind chance. The world which results bears the stamp of its creator. It is pronounced good. Creation is highly varied and this is no accident. God is depicted as powerful: just a word was enough to bring things into being.

The creation of human beings is separate from that of the animals. Humans are made stewards of the earth, looking after it on God's behalf. Humanity — male and female — is made in the "image", or likeness of God. The Bible presents men and women together as reflecting what God is like.

Points of interest
1. People differ in their opinions of what is meant by "the image of God". It might be humanity's capacity to love and to enter into relationships. It might be our ability to make moral choices.
2. The day of rest is part of the basis for the Sabbath day. Two reasons are given — the example of God resting after creation and the slaves being at rest after they left Egypt.

ELIJAH MEETS GOD
ELIJAH: EPISODE 3
1 Kings 19.1–18 ▶ *page 80*

A Christian perspective
In this story the writer emphasizes that God met Elijah in a way he was not expecting. He had had a

dramatic proof of God's presence on Mount Carmel, now he needed a different experience. He needed reassurance. God met Elijah at his point of need. Both wind and fire are often used as symbols of God's presence — but not in this case. In this story, God showed himself in a quiet whisper. In the Bible, meetings with God are not always the same type of experience. Elijah stood up for his faith on Mount Carmel but when the excitement was over, he came down with a bump. Jezebel sent him a death note and he fled into the desert to Sinai, a sacred area where Moses had received the Law.

Points of interest

1. The word Baal means Lord. The Israelites were to accept no one as Lord except God.
2. The desert is a place of retreat: in the Bible it is often a place to find God, and oneself. Significantly it is to Sinai that Elijah goes, the place where Moses met God in the burning bush, and where God gave the Law. It is in the wilderness, away from the anger of Jezebel, that Elijah meets God.

GOD THE SHEPHERD
Psalm 23 ▶ page 81

A Christian perspective
The psalmist likens God to a good shepherd. The important points to bring out are that the shepherd cares for and knows his sheep. He protects them and provides for them. See also "The Lost Sheep" (page 21), and "I am the Good Shepherd" (page 35). The picture in this poem changes from God as a shepherd to God as a host. The individual is seen as an honoured guest at a meal over which God presides.

Points of interest

1. Sheep were vitally important to the economy of ancient Israel. They provided meat and wool.
2. The eastern shepherd led his sheep to water and grass because pasture was scarce. The shepherd had to find suitable grazing first . He also protected the sheep from wild animals such as wolves, lions, and bears.
3. At night he put the sheep into a sheepfold, an area with a stone wall topped with thorns. The sheepfold had no door. The shepherd lay across the entrance to protect the sheep. He slept in his cloak, which was usually of thick camel hair. Jesus later described himself as a "door" or "gate" (page 35).
4. The shepherd carried a club, sometimes inset with bits of stone, to defend the sheep from wild animals. He also carried a stick with a curve at the end to rescue the sheep if they got in trouble or to guide them. He had a sling to scare away wild animals, and he carried a flask of oil to put on wounds if the sheep were hurt.
5. Life is often described as a "cup": it can be full of happiness or sorrow. The brimming cup is also the symbol of festivity.
6. Deep–sided valleys, whose sides were full of caves, were often the haunts of robbers and wild animals. This picture of a dangerous place, through which shepherds would sometimes pass, came to represent fear and dark experiences such as death. The Authorised Version of the Bible describes it as "the valley of the shadow of death".

GOD PROVIDES IN THE WILDERNESS
MOSES: EPISODE 7
Exodus 15.22–17.7 ▶ page 82

A Christian perspective
In this story, the writer emphasizes God providing when the Israelites were in need. They had forgotten how to survive as bedouin in the wilderness as they had been settled in Egypt for many generations. "Provider" is one of the titles of God. God provides for his people whether it be through the miraculous provision of manna or the everyday provision of food through "natural" processes.

Points of interest

1. The name "manna" is literally, "what is it?" or "what is its name?" in Hebrew.
2. Quail are very low–flying birds, and they flew over the camp. They would have been very easy to catch.
3. Lack of water was a perennial problem in the desert. There were oases and springs, and often the Israelites would camp by these for some time. It was not a constant march. The water from artesian wells is often bitter, because of the minerals which are washed into them.
4. The Israelites wandered between Egypt and Canaan for forty years, though Canaan is no great distance from the former. They became bedouin in the desert: they were not on a non–stop route march. The Israelites were condemned to stay in the desert for forty years because they did not trust God to lead them into the Promised Land. They had been frightened when they saw the size of the cities there.

5. The Israelites could not take the direct route to Canaan via the coast, as it was manned by Egyptian garrisons.

SOME TITLES OF GOD

Deuteronomy 1.31; 32.6, 10; 1 Samuel 2.3; Psalm 91.4; 18.2; Isaiah 49.15; 66.13; Romans 8.15–16; 1 Corinthians 4.5 ▶ *page 83*

A Christian perspective

The biblical writers likened God to a father. The father figure was one of authority, love, and care. It is a stronger image than that of twentieth–century fatherhood. God is also described as a mother, the emphasis being on her care and love. The two images go together. Both are images of care, but the emphasis is different. In an uncertain world, God was seen as a refuge, a tower, a fortress, and a shield. These are protective images of God. God is also described as a just judge who weighs the actions of humankind in his scales of justice. Judgement has two sides — the vindication and protection of the victim, and the punishment of the wrongdoer.

Points of interest

1. Jesus called God, "Abba", "Daddy". It is probably this word behind the word "Father" in the Lord's Prayer. For the Lord's Prayer, see page 62.
2. The "tower" could be the image of a defensive tower, such towers were sometimes set in city walls.

God the Creator

Genesis 1.1–2.4

In the beginning — before anything else existed — God made the heavens and the earth. But the earth was an unformed globe, with no life of any sort upon it. And there was water over its whole surface, and darkness everywhere. But there, in the darkness, was the Spirit of God, hovering over the waters.

Then God spoke. "Let there be light!" he commanded — and light sprang into being. God separated the light from the darkness — and so made the first day and the first night.

Next, God created the airy space around the earth, and he called it "sky". He trapped some of the earth's water into clouds in the sky, so that the cycles of dew, rain, and snow could begin. And this was done on the second day.

Then God gathered the waters on the earth into oceans, seas, lakes and rivers — and so the dry land appeared. And God was pleased with all he saw. "The land is ready now for green covering," he said, and he created a vast variety of trees and plants to clothe his new land. He was pleased with this, too, as he looked at the many shades of green, the brightly coloured flowers, the waving grass, and the rich fruits. And this was his work on the third day.

On the fourth day, God made the lights in the sky: he made a great light, the sun, to rule over the daytime, and a smaller one to glow in the night. Then he created thousands of stars. "All these lights will show when it is day or night, summer or winter," he said — and he was pleased with his work on the fourth day.

Then he knew that his earth was ready to receive living creatures. "I want the sea to be teeming with life — from tiny creatures to great whales. I want the sky to be filled with all kinds of birds — goldcrests and eagles, wrens and albatrosses." And so it all was. God looked closely at all of these creatures — and he was pleased with everything he saw. So the fifth day passed.

On the sixth day, God turned his attention to the land. He created all different kinds of animals — from the tiny shrew to the great elephant, animals living in the great jungles, and those who live in snow and ice. And again God was pleased with everything he had made.

And then God said, "I will now make humans, who will be like me and not just animals. They will love and speak and pray, and they will know me. They will look after my earth and its creatures." God created people like himself: male and female were both made by him. And he named them Adam and Eve and they were the first humans.

The sixth day ended. And on the seventh day God did no more work of creating, because he had made all he wanted to make, and he was completely satisfied with everything. So he ordered that the seventh day of the week was always to be spent in rest and recreation, because he had no more work to do on that first seventh day.

Elijah Meets God

ELIJAH: EPISODE 3

1 Kings 19.1–18

After God showed his great power on Mount Carmel and the rain had come again, Queen Jezebel sent a message to Elijah: "I am going to kill you because you have defeated Baal's prophets." Elijah panicked and ran away into the desert. He was very unhappy. Things were still not going right for him. "I might as well be dead for all the good I do," he moaned.

But God was listening. He sent Elijah food to strengthen him, and led him many miles to a lonely cave on a hillside. There he spoke to him: "What are you doing in the desert, Elijah?" he asked.

Elijah began his complaint. "I've always done my best for you God, but the Israelites have continually disobeyed you. They break down your altars and kill your prophets. Jezebel is trying to kill me now. I'm the only one left who follows you. I've had enough."

"Go outside," God answered. "I am going to show myself to you."

Suddenly a very strong wind tore by. It wrenched chunks of earth and stone off the hill and shattered them. Elijah cowered down. God was not in the wind! Fire suddenly raged all about him. He could feel its heat and its power, but he did not feel God's presence in it.

Then, as Elijah braced himself for the next trial, there came a gentle whisper. And Elijah recognized the voice of God. He covered his face and went out of the cave. God said again quietly, "What are you doing here, Elijah?" Elijah again listed his complaints.

Then God answered. "Listen to me, Elijah," he said. "Go back to your task, for I will defeat this evil king. I have chosen Elisha to work with you, and to be my special messenger after you. And remember you are not the only one who still loves me. There are 7,000 people in Israel who have refused to worship Baal, because they follow me."

So Elijah left the desert and returned to his work. When he felt discouraged again, he thought about the quiet voice of God, and remembered that many other people were still following God.

God the Shepherd

Psalm 23

The Lord is my shepherd,
I have everything I need.
As a shepherd leads his sheep into green fields
And brings them to a gently flowing stream,
So God leads me to the place where I can rest.
As a shepherd guides his flock along safe paths,
Keeping them free of danger,
So God guides me.
Even though I walk through deepest darkness,
I remember that you, God, are with me.
Therefore I will not be afraid
For you protect me,
As a shepherd protects his sheep with his staff and club.
You show my enemies how much you care for me
And treat me as your special guest.
My cup of happiness overflows.
I rejoice in your love and care of me which never fail,
And I know that I will be with you for ever.

God Provides in the Wilderness

MOSES: EPISODE 7

Exodus 15.22–17.7

The Israelites were grumbling again! "At least we had enough food to eat in Egypt," they moaned. "You've brought us all the way into this desert to starve to death." Poor Moses and Aaron! They reminded the people that God had provided water for them when they were thirsty, so surely he would provide food. But it was no good. The Israelites still moaned on and on. They were hungry!

God knew his people had no food. He told Moses that he was going to send them meat and bread to eat. Moses hurried to tell the people.

"God has heard you all grumbling. He is going to show you again that he is looking after you. In the mornings, he will send bread to you. You are to collect enough to last you through the day. You must not take away any more except on the day before the Sabbath. Then you must collect enough for two days, because God does not want you gathering food on his day of rest. Remember! Every other day you are to collect bread for just one day. Then, in the evenings, God will send you some meat."

That evening the people waited. Would God send anything? Could he? They still didn't believe him, even though they had seen him do many incredible things in the past. Then, suddenly someone shouted "Look! There are flocks of birds coming this way!" And the birds — quite small ones, called quail — landed right in the camp, so the people were able to catch them easily. "Now we'll see if the bread arrives!" they thought.

Next morning, after the sun had dried up the dew, they could see white flakes of something on the ground. "What is it?" they shouted to each other.

Then one of them dared to taste it. "It's good!" he shouted. "It tastes of honey! This is the 'bread' that God has sent for us." So they all tried it. It was good! They all collected some, as Moses had said. The next day the ground was covered with new, fresh manna. God had kept his promise. On the day before the Sabbath, the people collected an extra day's supply, as God had told them to.

The Israelites travelled in the desert for forty years and for all that time God always sent them manna. But they still grumbled, and still didn't trust him to look after them. The next time they ran out of water, they turned against God again. "Why have you brought us out here?" they shouted at Moses. "We will die of thirst! If God is really here with us, why are we so thirsty?" So, once again, God had to show his people that he was looking after them. There was a great rock standing in that part of the desert, and God told Moses to hit it with his staff. Immediately fresh, sweet water flowed out of the rock itself, and the Israelites drank deeply.

So God patiently cared for his people as they struggled on.

Some Titles of God

God as a Father

The Lord your God has cared for you in the desert just as a father carries and cares for his son. (Deuteronomy 1.31)

God is your Father: he made you and he rescued you. He carried you on his back as an eagle carries its young. (Deuteronomy 32.6, 10)

With the help of God's Spirit, we can cry to God, "Father, my Father!" for God calls us his children. (Romans 8.15–16)

God as Mother

Do you think it is possible for a mother to forget or to ignore her own child — the child to whom she gave birth, for whom she has fed and cared? Even if a mother did forget her child, I will never forget you. It is as if I have your name written on the palms of my hands, where I can see it all the time. (Isaiah 49.15)

God will look after you as a mother bird gathers her young chicks under her wings, to protect them and keep them warm with her feathers. So will God look after you. (Psalm 91.4)

Imagine a mother nursing her child. The child is upset and crying and she is holding him tightly, whispering to him, making everything all right for him again. So will the Lord comfort you and care for you. And you will be happy again. (Isaiah 66.13)

God as a Shield and Fortress

The Lord is my rock, my fortress and my deliverer. I run to him for shelter. He is my shield and my rescuer. He protects me as if he is a strong tower. (Psalm 18.2)

God as Judge

God is a God who knows: he judges what people have done, weighing them and their deeds in his scales. (1 Samuel 2.3)

You should not pass judgement on anyone before the right time comes. Final judgement belongs to the Lord. He is the one who knows the secrets of a person's heart and the hidden thoughts of people's minds. On that day, everyone will receive from God the praise they deserve. (1 Corinthians 4.5)

Icons

Some Christians use icons in their worship of God.

An icon is a special picture, but it is far more than a picture.

All parts of God's creation are used to make an icon:

Vegetable — icons are painted on wood. The finished icon is brushed with linseed oil to preserve it.

Mineral — the wood is covered with "gesso", which is powdered stone mixed with water and glue. Many of the colours used are mineral .

Animal — the colours are mixed with egg yolk. Gelatin is used to seal the wood and animal–based glue is used in the making of gesso.

Human — last of all, human creativity is added.

In Deuteronomy, the Israelites are told to worship God with everything they have got — with all their heart and soul, all their mind and strength. Icons also try to use all parts of creation to worship God.

Activity

• Make your own picture that uses animal, vegetable, and mineral materials, and human creativity. For example: wool could be used for the animal element. Please check all the items you want to use with your teacher to make sure they are suitable and safe.

God's Eyes — A Mexican Decoration

Christians describe God in many ways. They describe him as all–loving, all–powerful, always present and all–knowing. We see part of a situation, Christians believe God sees the whole. These Mexican "God's eyes" can be a reminder to Christians that God sees all and is all–knowing.

Activity

- Take two straws. Make a small hole in the centre of one of them, so that you can thread the other one through it.

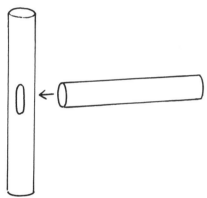

- Take some coloured wool and fasten the end to the back of your cross shape with a small piece of sellotape.

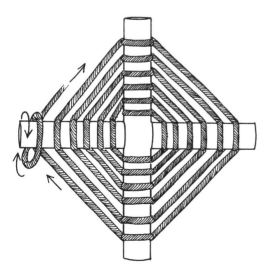

- Carefully wind the wool as shown.
  If you wish, you can use several colours to make your "God's eye" colourful.

Celebrating God the Provider

Read the story called "God Provides in the Wilderness" on page 82.

Christians do not have a special celebration in order to remember this story, but Jews do. Each year, Jewish people celebrate God providing for them in the wilderness in the festival of Succoth.

Succoth

During this festival, a shelter called a "Sukkah" is made in each family's garden. Sometimes the roof is taken off the shed, and the shed is then used as the "Sukkah". For a week, meals are eaten outside in the shelter and prayers are said there. The shelter is decorated with paper fruits, and pictures of the wandering in the wilderness are displayed on the walls. The roof of the shelter is covered with branches, but with gaps so that people can see the stars, because people remember that the children of Israel did not have fixed homes for many years, but were wandering bedouin.

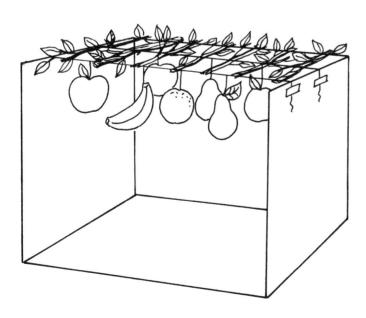

Activity

- Find out all you can about the festival of Succoth, what it says about God, and about its place in the Jewish faith.

- As a group, make a small Sukkah from a crisp box. Draw tiny pictures to decorate the walls. Use some branches to cover the top. Make some fruits to hang.

- As a group, prepare a presentation to explain to the rest of the class what a Sukkah is, and the story behind it.

A Multi–sided Shape

Activity

- Make a shape with six or more sides.

- Make a pattern or "net" first and test out your design in scrap paper/card before you make your best copy.

  Example:

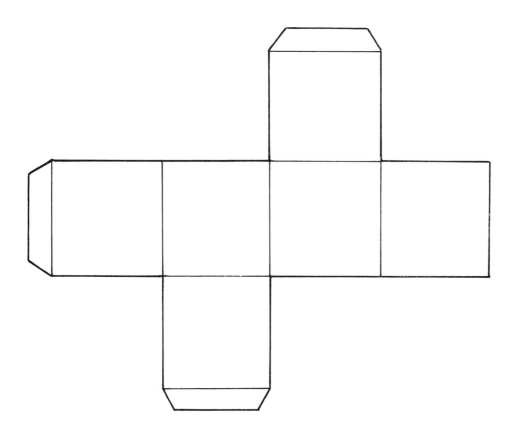

- Christians have many descriptions of God. From the stories on pages 81 and 83 can you write a different description of God on each side of your shape? If you wish, you can draw a symbol or picture on each side of your shape, instead of writing the different descriptions. Each description should explain part of God's character as Christians understand it.

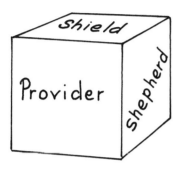

- When you have finished, suspend your shape. How are you going to do this?

THE HOLY SPIRIT

Understanding the biblical ideas

Christians describe the Holy Spirit as the third person of the Trinity. He is a person, not an "it", not just a force or influence. God, though one, is expressed in three forms: God the Father (creator and sustainer of the world), God the Son, Jesus (God in human form showing what God is like), and God the Holy Spirit (God in action or God with us now). With children, it is sometimes easier to call God the Holy Spirit "God the helper", "God in action", or "God the invisible friend".

Pentecost, the celebration of the coming of the Holy Spirit, is the birthday of the Church, the birthday of the whole Christian family. It is one of the three major Christian festivals, the others being Christmas and Easter.

The Holy Spirit is sometimes likened to wind. A noise like a rushing wind occurs in the story in Acts 2. The Holy Spirit is also like the wind in that you cannot see the wind, but you can see the results of its power. You can see the power of the Spirit in people's lives, changing them, but you can't see the Holy Spirit.

The words used for Spirit in the Bible, "*pneuma*" and "*ruach*", both mean breath or wind (hence our words pneumonia, pneumatic, etc.) God gives Adam the breath of life, and he becomes a living being. Ezekiel's dry bones come together, but they do not live until the breath enters them. The Holy Spirit is the life–giving Spirit.

The Holy Spirit is likened to fire. In the story of the coming of the Holy Spirit, the disciples see what look like tongues of fire. Fire is a cleansing agent: just as heat kills germs, so the Holy Spirit changes people, removing wrong.

The Holy Spirit is likened to water that cleanses and refreshes. Jesus refers to the Holy Spirit as "living" water, meaning a spring or stream. The symbol of water is used because water gives life and water cleanses and refreshes. The cleansing aspect links the Holy Spirit with baptism.

Introducing the passages

Talk about invisible friends with the children. If possible, read a story about a child with an invisible friend. Christians believe they have a real invisible friend in the Holy Spirit. Introduce the idea of the Spirit as an invisible friend and comforter. This can be found on the page headed "Understanding the Holy Spirit".

Discuss invisible forces such as wind and electricity. Demonstrate some of these, making sure everything used is safe. Introduce the story of the coming of the Holy Spirit, who gave the disciples a new sort of power.

Ask a parent to bring in a baby. Talk with the children about starting life and the life the baby has ahead of it. Introduce the idea of a fresh start. Tell the story of Nicodemus.

Explore how we breathe and why air is needed for life. Read the story called "Dry Bones".

Bring in some presents. Discuss some of the tangible presents we receive in life and follow this by looking at the "Gifts of the Holy Spirit".

Bring in a selection of fruits and talk about fruit as the harvest of the plant. Look at the "Fruits of the Spirit", these fruits being the harvest of a relationship with God.

Other useful passages

"Jesus is Baptized", page 31. In this story, the Holy Spirit gives Jesus the power he needs for his ministry.

"Jesus says Goodbye", page 52. In this story, Jesus tells the disciples to wait for the Holy Spirit to come.

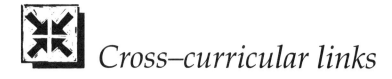

Cross–curricular links

English
- Discuss baptism and what it means to different denominations. (1)
- Discuss the various ways water is used: giving life, cleansing, and refreshing. (1)
- Invite clergy from different churches to talk about baptism or write letters requesting information. (1)
- Imagine that you are out in a strong gale. How do you feel battling against the elements? Write a poem describing your physical and emotional feelings. (3)
- Explore Ezekiel's vision of dry bones in drama. (1)

Mathematics
- Draw doves in a circle to symbolize the gifts of the Spirit. How many will you need? (1, 4)
- Measure and record the wind speed and direction on a wind rose (a diagrammatic record of wind direction). This can be done using information technology, e.g. the software "Display Data" available from Resource, Doncaster, DNP 4PY. Is there a link between the force of the wind and its direction? Look for a pattern. (1, 2, 5)

Science
- Make a model or a vehicle which requires wind energy to make it work, e.g. windmill, land yacht. Which model/vehicle works the best? Can you devise a fair test to prove this? (1, 4) (TAT 1, 2)

Music
- Investigate how wind instruments work. Make a simple wind instrument and find different ways of changing the sound. (2)

Technology
- Can you design and make an instrument for measuring the wind? Test your design. How can you improve upon your initial design? (1, 2)
- Can you design and make a weathercock to show the direction of the wind? (1, 2)

Geography
- Use research material such as an index, globe, and a map of the world to plot where Christianity has spread today. (1)
- Using relevant maps, look at regions which require irrigation to make the land fertile and areas which are suffering from drought or monsoons. (1)
- Investigate the power of the wind by using the Beaufort Scale. (1)

Art
- Make a model out of clay to show someone struggling to walk against the wind. How would the body look? (1)
- Paint an abstract picture or make a collage to show how high winds make you feel. (1)

History
- Look at the spread of Christianity and link this in with History units on:
  1. "Invaders and Settlers" — the growth of Christianity.
  2. "Victorians" — the missionary movement. (1, 2, 3)

PE/Dance
- Think about the qualities of the wind, fire, dove, and water. These are all symbols of the Holy Spirit. Choose one symbol to explore in dance. (KS 1/2)

DRY BONES
Ezekiel 37.1–14 ▶ *page 94*

A Christian perspective
In this story, God promises to revive the hope of his people by a vision of the Spirit bringing to life dead bones. All the hopes of the people are dead — so dead that they are like bleached bones. The Spirit brings the bones together again and breathes life into them. Christians believe this same spirit is active today, bringing a different type of life. The wind symbolizes power. The Hebrew word for spirit also means breath, the means of life.

Points of interest
1. Many of the people had been taken away captive to Babylon. For them, it seemed like the Egyptian slavery all over again. They saw no future. Ezekiel the prophet had been one of the first captured when the Babylonians creamed off all the leaders in order to deprive the people of possible leadership in a rebellion. Babylon was looked upon as the graveyard of many nations.
2. Psalm 137 expresses the despair of the exiles.

Teacher resource
Material on the Iona Community (see page 100) can be obtained from: Wild Goose Publications, The Pearce Institute, 840 Govan Road, Glasgow G51 3UT (041 445 4561).

NICODEMUS VISITS JESUS
John 3.1–21 ▶ *page 95*

A Christian perspective
The Bible likens the Spirit to wind because wind is both powerful and invisible. He is likened to breath because the Spirit gives life just as ordinary breath does. Starting life as a friend of God is described as being born all over again. It is having a fresh start with the help of the Spirit. Christians see the Spirit as an invisible friend and helper.

Points of interest
1. Nicodemus was part of the ruling council of the Jews, the Sanhedrin. He was a secret disciple, though he publicly defended Jesus in the Sanhedrin, and he also helped Joseph of Arimathea to bury Jesus.
2. Nicodemus was a sincere man who was trying to understand. He kept the Jewish Law and was surprised when Jesus said that being God's friend depended on making a fresh start with the help of the Spirit, not just on keeping the Law.

THE HOLY SPIRIT COMES
Acts 2 ▶ *page 96*

A Christian perspective
This story follows on from the story of the ascension (page 52). An important point for Christians is that the coming of the Holy Spirit fulfilled a promise. Hundreds of years earlier, prophets such as Joel had predicted this. Ten days beforehand, Jesus had told the disciples to wait for the Holy Spirit.

In the Bible, flames are often a symbol of the presence of God. In this case, they represent the Holy Spirit who for Christians is "God in action". Wind was the symbol of power. In this story, the Holy Spirit changes the disciples from frightened men into brave preachers.

Points of interest
1. The story takes place at Pentecost, a Jewish festival held fifty days after Passover. Pentecost is a harvest festival when thanks are said for the wheat crop and also for the giving of the Law.
2. The special king or the Messiah, had been expected for hundreds of years. Many people expected a warrior who would throw out the Romans, or, at least, a great leader of some sort. For most people, a teacher who told them how to love their enemies and who died the death of a criminal was not the type of Messiah they were expecting.

3. The disciples spoke in many languages. The people listening were Jews from many different countries. They would have spoken many different native languages, though the Jews would also have spoken either Greek or Aramaic.

UNDERSTANDING THE HOLY SPIRIT
A selection from John 14–16; 1 Corinthians 12; Galatians 5.22–23 ▶ *page 97*

A Christian perspective
Christians see the Holy Spirit as the replacement for the earthly presence of Jesus. He is also seen as the gift–bringer. The Holy Spirit is sometimes called the "Comforter" which can also be translated as "Champion". It literally means "someone who is called alongside to defend you". Christians see the Holy Spirit as an unseen friend and helper.

Each Christian is given different gifts in order to share them: they are not a private possession. The gifts are practical, enabling people to live as Christians.

Fruit is the result of the life of the tree. By the fruit, people know what sort of tree it is. In the same way, a relationship with God bears "fruit" in certain actions and qualities. Growth in these nine areas of life is evidence of a friendship with God.

The "fruit of the Spirit" is singular: it could be translated "harvest" but it has nine different aspects. With children, it might be easier to refer to nine separate "fruits" which are qualities and actions which should be the result of a relationship with God; the "harvest"of that relationship.

Point of interest
Love is the primary fruit. Joy is a happiness which is independent of circumstances. Kindness and goodness are very similar and both practical. Self–control means control achieved without outside constraints. Peace is an inward reality which should result in an outward difference in behaviour. Biblical peace is a broad word which also indicates a certain wholeness and health within relationships and the world. Patience is the ability to endure. Faithfulness can be faithfulness to God, holding fast to "the faith", or steadfastness under difficult circumstances. In this context it probably means trustworthiness. Gentleness or humility is not putting oneself down: neither is it a spineless lack of resistance to evil. It is the opposite of anger; it is a gentleness that promotes harmony.

Dry Bones

Ezekiel 37.1–14

When the people of Israel were taken away as slaves from their own country into Babylon, many of them felt that God must have abandoned them. But he used several people to bring them his messages, to encourage them, and to tell them to trust him. One of these messengers was Ezekiel. He himself was one of the captives. God gave him a series of visions or pictures — to help him to explain to the Israelites what God would do in the future, when he would restore his people to happiness in their own land. One of these visions tells us about the Holy Spirit and his work. Here is what Ezekiel said:

"God took me to a great valley, and the ground there was covered with old dried–up bones. God asked me, 'Can these bones come to life again, Ezekiel?'

"I don't know," I answered. "Only you can know the answer to that, Lord."

"Then God said, 'I will make these bones live. I will clothe them in tendons and in flesh, and cover them with skin. I will make them alive. Tell them that I will do all this, so that they will know that I am God.'

"I did as he told me: I shouted all this to the dead, dry bones. And they started to move. There was a rattling and a rasping as they joined together. Then muscle and skin grew on them — but they were not alive.

"So God told me how to bring life into them: 'Speak to the wind — to the breath of life — to the Spirit,' he said. When I did this, breath entered the bodies, and they lived and stood up.

"Then God explained all this to me. 'The Israelite people are like those bones, Ezekiel. They believe that everything is over for them, that they will die in captivity, and that Israel herself is dead. Tell them what you have seen. Tell them that I will bring them back to life. My Spirit will live in them, and they will return to their own country. And then they will know that I am still their God.'"

Nicodemus Visits Jesus

John 3.1–21

Nicodemus crept through the sleeping city, taking care that no one saw him. If the other members of the Council found out whom he'd been to see, he would be in great trouble. He was relieved when he reached home at last and hurriedly locked the door. Now he could relax and think about what Jesus had said.

He had admired Jesus for a long time, and had wanted to find out more about him. He felt that the other Jewish leaders were mistaken when they condemned Jesus as a trouble maker. But Nicodemus was not brave enough to go to Jesus openly. Just recently, Jesus had upset the Council (and many other people) by throwing out all the salesmen and moneychangers from the Temple Courts! So Nicodemus had gone secretly to Jesus in the middle of the night.

Jesus had seemed to understand why Nicodemus had come at such an odd time. He had been pleased to talk to him; but the things he had said had confused and puzzled Nicodemus.

Jesus had said, "No one can be God's friend unless he starts life all over again."

Nicodemus found that impossible to understand. He realized that Jesus knew just why he had come — to find out how to please God — even though Nicodemus had not told him. But what did he mean by "starting life all over again"?

"How can anyone start life again?" he'd asked Jesus. "A grown man can't become a baby again."

Jesus had explained what he meant. "Becoming a friend of God is like being born all over again. It is a completely fresh start. The Spirit of God behaves like the wind. We can hear the wind, and it blows wherever it wants to. But we don't know where the wind comes from or where it goes next. It is like this with the Spirit's work. You cannot see the Spirit working inside someone," Jesus had concluded.

"So I've got plenty to think about," thought Nicodemus, as he settled down that night.

The Holy Spirit Comes

Acts 2

After Jesus had left them, the disciples waited in Jerusalem, as he had told them to. One day, while they were all together, there came a sudden loud noise filling the room, like the roaring of a very strong wind. As they looked at each other in amazement, they saw what seemed to be flames, moving in the air, until they rested on each disciple without hurting them. The Holy Spirit had come as Jesus had said he would! They felt his power within them, and they were immediately able to speak in many new languages with his help. They began to praise God loudly, thanking him for keeping this promise. They shouted so loudly, in fact, that soon a crowd had gathered to see what was happening.

Now, in this crowd, there were Jews from other countries, who had come to Jerusalem to worship at the Temple. Each of these people now realized, to their great surprise, that he could hear his own language being spoken by one or other of the apostles. "But these men are Galileans, surely?" they queried. "How can they — just ordinary people — know so many different languages?"

"Because they are drunk!" some of the crowd answered sarcastically. "Their drunken ramblings just sound like other languages."

Then Peter stood up where all the crowd could see him. "No, we're not drunk!" he shouted. "What you are seeing here is a prophecy being fulfilled. You know that years and years ago the prophet Joel wrote that God would pour out his Holy Spirit on many people — that is what is happening today!"

The crowd were eager now to hear more, so Peter went on to explain about Jesus' life and death. "God has now raised Jesus to life again," he went on. "We have all seen him. Listen to me. That man Jesus, who was killed in this city, is the special king you have been waiting for!"

Many of the people listening came to believe that Jesus was the special king and they asked Peter what they should do. "Just ask God to forgive you and be baptized," replied Peter. And that day 3,000 people became followers of Jesus.

Understanding the Holy Spirit

A selection from John 14–16; 1 Corinthians 12; Galatians 5.22–23

Jesus often spoke about the Holy Spirit. Here are some of the things he said: "Don't worry, I will not leave you all alone. When I am gone, the Holy Spirit will come. God will send him to stay with you always. He is the Counsellor: he will guide you and give you good advice. He is the Comforter: he will always be with you and will help you when you need him. He is the Teacher: he will remind you about things I have said to you. He always tells the truth, he cannot lie. (John 14.18, 25–28; 16.7, 13)

Paul Explains the Gifts of the Spirit

The Spirit gives different gifts to people to enable them to help each other — gifts such as wisdom, faith, and the ability to heal people. All of these gifts come from the same Holy Spirit. They help people to serve in many different ways.

People, with their different gifts, should work together. It is as if each person is a part of a body. The parts of a human body all work together very well, even though they all do different jobs, and all of them are needed. It would be no good if the ear decided it wasn't really a necessary part of the body just because it wasn't an eye. It is needed as an ear. After all, how would a person get on if his whole body was just an eye? This means that the head cannot say "I don't need you, feet," because it obviously does need them. The parts of the body work together so closely, and are so necessary to each other, that if one part is hurt, then the whole body feels the pain.

It is like this with the Christian "body" of believers. Each "part" or person, with his or her own special gift, is needed. No one person should make fun of another one, just because they have different talents. And if one person is hurt, then all the other members of the group should share their pain. If one person is joyful then people should share that happiness as well. So we should not be jealous or scornful of other people's gifts, but should use our own as well as we can, to help each other. (1 Corinthians 12.1–31)

The Fruit of the Spirit, from a letter by Paul

Just as trees and plants grow good fruit, so the Holy Spirit produces "fruit" in the lives of Christians: fruit such as love, joy, peace, patience, kindness and goodness, faithfulness, gentleness and self–control. All these will please God and will help other people. (Galatians 5.22–23)

Wool Winding

Read the story "The Holy Spirit Comes" on page 96.

The Holy Spirit is described in various ways. He is likened to fire, to wind, and to water. Find the places where the Spirit is pictured as fire and wind in this story.

Activity

- Choose one of these descriptions of the Holy Spirit: wind, fire or water.

- Collect lots of pieces of knitting wool. The pieces do not have to be very long.

- Choose a selection of coloured wools which you think express the description you have chosen. If you choose fire, you might choose reds, yellows, oranges, and golds.

- Take a strip of card 10 cm long and 2 cm wide. Wind double–sided tape around it.

- Press the end of one piece of wool on to the double–sided tape, and start winding. Cut the wool and press the end into the tape when you have used as much of that colour as you want. Start the next colour in the same way. Cover all of your strip of card.

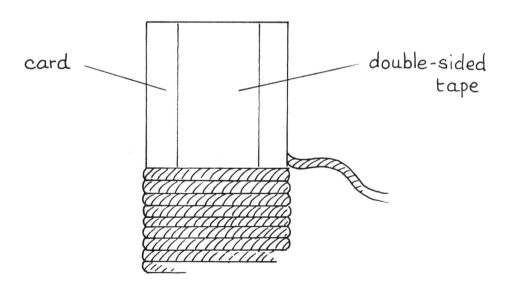

card — double-sided tape

Things to think about

Which colours would you use for water?
Which colours would you use for wind?
Which colours would you use for fire?

Colours often express how we feel. We say people are "green with envy" or "red with anger". The Church uses colour to express various events and beliefs. Find out from a Christian which colours are traditionally used at Pentecost.

Symbols of the Spirit

Wind, fire and dove are all symbols of the Holy Spirit.

Look though each of the following stories to find the symbol of the Holy Spirit.

"Dry Bones", page 94; "Jesus is Baptized", page 31;
"Nicodemus Visits Jesus", page 95; "The Holy Spirit Comes", page 96.

The dove is often used by Christians today to represent the Holy Spirit. You can find it on cards, banners, stained glass and paintings. In which story does the dove appear? Why do you think a dove was chosen rather than any other bird?

Celtic Christians used the wild goose as a symbol of the Holy Spirit. Why do you think they chose the wild goose instead of a dove? Discuss this with a friend.

® ™ The Wild Goose is the registered trademark of Wild Goose Publications of the Iona Community. Reproduced by permission.

Reaping the Fruit Harvest

Every year, the farmers gather in the fruit harvest. Fruit is the result of the life of the tree. Trees may not look as if there is much going on inside, but inside the leaves and trunk a lot is going on. The result of all that activity is fruit.

It is similar with Christians. You cannot see a person's relationship with God, but you can see the results in their lives.

Group activity

- Write down some of the fruits that are harvested each year.

- Choose nine fruits to make from this list.

- Share out the fruits so that each person makes one from sugar paper or card.

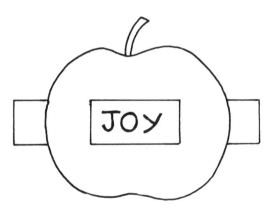

- Now read about the "fruits" of the Holy Spirit. You will find these on the page headed "Understanding the Holy Spirit" on page 97.

- Share out the different "fruits" of the Spirit so that each person has one to attach to their fruit.

- How could you put the name of the fruit of the Spirit on the fruit you have made?

Wind Words

Read the story of Nicodemus on page 95.

Kites come in many different shapes.

- Make a kite from tissue and strips of card as a centre piece for a display. Make brightly coloured ribbons for the tail. Remember kites can be many different shapes.

- Think up words to describe the wind. How could you put wind words on your kite?

Think about it

Kites show the power of the wind. They make an invisible power visible, because we can see the power of the wind in the flight of the kite. Christians liken the Holy Spirit to wind, because he has the power to change people. You cannot see the Spirit but you can see the changes he makes in people.

You might like to design a kite which flies. If you do, fly it with an adult. Make sure you wear gloves and fly it in a safe place away from power cables.

STANDING UP FOR WHAT YOU BELIEVE

Understanding biblical ideas

The Bible is full of characters who stood up for what they believed. Sometimes this meant they were persecuted or even died for their faith. Both Old and New Testaments contain stories of people who died for their faith.

In the Old Testament, the three friends are sent to the fiery furnace because they will not bow down to Nebuchadnezzer's idol. God is with them in the fire but they do not escape the experience. Daniel faces the lions rather than give up praying. Jeremiah faces a lifetime of persecution, including being thrown down a pit and left to rot. Elijah has to run for his life from Jezebel and feels he is the only person left still worshipping God.

In the New Testament, John the Baptist suffers at the hands of Herod, being decapitated in Machaerus prison. Stephen is the first Christian to die for his faith, being stoned to death outside Jerusalem. Paul persecutes Christians, throwing them into prison whenever possible. Peter is imprisoned and probably eventually died for his faith in Rome. Herod had the disciple James beheaded publically. John, the author of the book of Revelation, was exiled on the island of Patmos. Paul, after his conversion to Christianity, endured a catalogue of suffering but considered it worthwhile.

Suffering is looked upon as normal. In a world in which evil abounds, those who stand up for what they believe must expect to suffer. Life is a battle between good and evil, and Christians are told to equip themselves for the fight.

Introducing the passages

Listen to *The Daniel Jazz* by H Chappell (Novello) if possible. Discuss Daniel's situation. What do you do when someone tells you not to do something you know is right, or if they tell you to do something you know is wrong? Introduce the stories of Daniel and the three friends in the fire. Discuss the difficulties people face when they stand up for what they believe. Look at some modern people who have suffered, such as the poet Irina Ratashinskya, Desmond Tutu, and Allan Boesak. Look at some of the hardships Paul endured.

Explore the things that enable people to stand firm in difficult times. Look at the Christian "Armour for the Battle".

Talk about how people feel about their persecutors. How do we feel about people who give us a rough time? Look at the example of Stephen. Please stress that bullying is not to be put up with. Standing up for what you believe includes standing up for the right of every person to be treated as a special, valued creation of God. That includes oneself!

Other useful passages

"Elijah and the Prophets of Baal", Book 2, page 79–80.

"Elijah meets God", page 80.

"Paul meets Jesus", Book 2, page 64.

"Three friends in the Fire", Book 2, page 78.

"The Death of John the Baptist", Book 2, page 34.

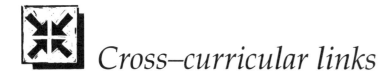

Cross–curricular links

English

- Debate a contentious modern day issue such as factory farming or "green" issues. Marshal your arguments, be prepared to speak for and against the motion. (1)
- Read *Mrs Frisby and the Rats of Nihm* by R O'Brien (Puffin). What stands are being taken on major issues? Précis the attitude of Mrs Frisby to the world. (2, 3)
- Have a "Balloon Debate" — there are six famous people in the balloon which needs lightening. Who will go first, second, etc.? Research your character and give your reasons for not being jettisoned. (1, 2)
- Read the story of Maximillian Kolbe (a simple version "Fanciszek and Father Maximillian" is published by The Catholic Truth Society). Why did he give his life? Can you write a speech for him that gives his motive? (2, 3)
- Read the list of hardships which Paul suffered. Imagine you have a camera. In your "mind's eye" take a photograph of one incident which happened to Paul, e.g. a shipwreck. Describe your photograph in detail. (2, 3)
- What is the difference between physical strength and "inner strength"? (1)

Music

- Look at famous hymns and songs such as "We will overcome", and "Onward Christian Soldiers", and other songs which give a message of protest. How do songs like these influence the singer and the listener? (2)
- Playing a keyboard as a backing track compose a rap about an issue you care about. Look at the hymn "Stand up, Stand up for Jesus" — devise strong percussion to accompany it. Which instruments would you choose and why? Work in groups and share your composition. (1)

Personal and Social Education

- Is it always wrong to tell a lie? Discuss *The Diary of Ann Frank*. What about white lies? Is it permissible to lie to save someone. What about lying to save someone's feelings? (EAT 1)
- Explore ideas such as "strength of character" and the difficulties of standing up for your beliefs when people laugh or torment. (EAT 1)

Mathematics

- Collect information along the lines of "Standing up and being counted" — any data will do as long as it is suitable for your class. (5)
- Show your information in graphic form. Use information technology to do a survey on a topical controversial issue. (5)

Science and Technology

- What is strength? Who is the strongest in the class? Devise your own safe activities and a strength metre. Record your results. Make a fair and safe strength test. Discuss how to do this. (SAT 1, 4) (TAT 1, 2)

History

- Look at the lives of famous people who stood up for other people's rights or their own faith, e.g. Oscar Romero, Evangeline Jebb (Save the Children Fund). In each case, look at what they stood up for and why. What effect did this have on their society both at the time and in later times? (1, 2)
- Draw a time line of this century. Research ten significant figures and issues and their relative importance for our lives today. (1)

Art

- Read your description of your imaginary photograph and try to draw the scene on that photograph. (1)
- Using the life story of one of the historical figures you have researched, draw a story board for a five minute documentary on their life. (1)

DANIEL AND THE LIONS
DANIEL: EPISODE 3
Daniel 6 ▶ *page 107*

A Christian perspective

This story depicts God as a powerful and faithful God. Daniel was prepared to carry on serving God, even though he knew what the consequences of that might be. He did not know whether God would save him. He was prepared to stand by what he believed, even if he wasn't rescued.

Points of interest

1. Daniel prayed three times a day facing Jerusalem, the "city of God" which had been destroyed by Nebuchadnezzar. Jews usually stood to pray, but Daniel knelt.
2. Darius was the king of the Persian Empire. Daniel, a Jew, had been taken to Babylon when a

young man and had served under Nebuchadnezzar, but eventually the Babylonian Empire had fallen to Persia (modern Iran) and Daniel, as a slave, had changed hands.

3. The laws of the Persians could not be revoked, so Darius' hands were tied. The same situation crops up in the story of Esther.
4. Under the Babylonians, the death penalty was often carried out by fire. Daniel's friends had been thrown into a furnace. Fire was sacred to the Persians, so lions were used instead— amongst other methods. (The Persians were one of the first peoples to use crucifixion.) Lions were kept for hunting, not just for execution purposes.

JEREMIAH IN THE PIT
Jeremiah 38.1–13 ▶ *page 108*

A Christian perspective
The Bible does not paint a rosy picture in which messages from God are always well received. Some prophets suffered because of the message they delivered: Jeremiah was one of them. Jeremiah delivered these messages for about forty years. He was opposed by almost every sector of the population from workers to kings. Despite opposition, Jeremiah refused to change his message. He stood up for his faith, even if it meant standing up to the king.

Points of interest
1. The name Ebed–Melech means servant of the king.
2. Jeremiah was considered a traitor because he foretold the occupation of his country and the fall of Jerusalem.
3. The king was a weak man. He allowed Jeremiah to be imprisoned but was reluctant to kill him, as killing a prophet of God was a terrible thing to do, and he had an almost superstitious fear of doing this. Herod later felt the same about John the Baptist, whom he kept in prison but was reluctant to kill.

STEPHEN DIES
Acts 6.1–8.1 ▶ *page 109*

A Christian perspective
Stephen was the first Christian recorded as dying for his faith. He stood up for his beliefs, even though he knew they would get him into trouble with the authorities. Stephen's words of forgiveness are similar to those of Jesus, who said, "Father forgive them; they don't know what they are doing."

Points of interest
1. This was the beginning of an early persecution of which Saul (Paul) was a part. This persecution was instrumental in spreading the Christian Church. Most of the later persecution was instigated by the Roman government, but at this early stage the Romans ignored the Christians. The Romans had granted religious toleration to the Jews, and they saw Christianity as a sect of Judaism.
2. The Jews may not have had the authority to impose the death penalty at the time, and so Stephen's death may have been a "lynching".
3. "Remember" is a strong word in Hebrew; it includes action. "Forgiveness" was God "forgetting" and not punishing.
4. The early Church in Jerusalem pooled its wealth. The Greek–speaking Christians, however, had complained that their widows were not getting their fair share of food, so seven men were appointed to distribute it fairly. Stephen was one of those men. All of the seven men have Greek names. It seems the church was trying hard to be fair by putting in charge the group that felt discriminated against.

PAUL STANDS FIRM
2 Corinthians 11.16–33 ▶ *page 110*

A Christian perspective
It is not the places Paul visited, or even the hardships that he endured, that are important to Christians. What matters is what drove the man to travel such distances under terrible conditions and endure such hardships. The message must have been important to him!

Points of interest
1. On one occasion, Paul was shipwrecked and landed on the island of Malta. This happened because he was travelling too late in the season. Normally, shipping ceased through the winter.
2. Paul was whipped by both the Romans and the Jews. Five times he had the thirty–nine stripes from the Jews. They were allowed to give forty but Jews, out of respect for the Law, gave one less to prevent them accidentally breaking the Law if they lost count. Paul could have refused this punishment, as he was a Roman citizen, but he stood by his identity as a Jew. Three times he was beaten by the Romans: as a Roman citizen, he was actually exempt from this.
3. Paul was stoned. This could indicate the Jewish death penalty and could have been an unauthorized "lynching" as the Jews probably

did not have the death penalty at the time. Alternatively it could be mob violence "throwing stones".

4. Paul worked as a tentmaker or leather worker to support himself. All Jewish men were taught a trade, even if, like Paul they had a university education.

ARMOUR FOR THE BATTLE

Ephesians 6.10–20 ▶ *page 111*

A Christian perspective

The point of this section is that Christians believe they are involved in a battle, but they are not expected to fight alone or without protection.

Points of interest

1. The belt of truth. Jesus described himself as "the Truth" when he said, "I am the Way, the Truth and the Life". Christians are meant to reflect God and Jesus in their behaviour, being honest and expressing the "truths" they believe about God in their lives. The belt identified a soldier on duty.

2. The breastplate of righteousness. The breastplate covered the vital organs. "Righteousness" is right behaviour and right relationships, with God, and with others.

3. Shoes. These were the caliga, the half boot which enabled the soldier to complete long marches.

4. The Good News (gospel) of peace. This is the peace in friendship with God, and peace that should be spread on earth.

5. The shield of faith. The shield covered most of the body and could be locked with other shields to form a "tortoise" — a defensive wall and ceiling of shields used primarily in siege warfare. The shield had the name of the soldier on it and that of his commanding officer. Faith is trust in God.

6. The helmet of salvation. "Salvation" is being rescued from wrong. The plume on a soldier's helmet aided recognition of him in battle.

7. The sword was a short, stabbing weapon. The Word of God was often likened to a sharp, two–edged sword which went straight to the heart of the matter.

Daniel and the Lions

DANIEL: EPISODE 3

Daniel 6

Daniel's enemies waited impatiently. Was it time yet? Would the plan succeed? They had worked it out carefully. Daniel was becoming too powerful. King Darius was about to promote him again — to make him more powerful than any of them! They could not let that happen. For weeks they had tried to discover something that Daniel had done wrong, to turn Darius against him. But they couldn't find anything! Daniel didn't seem to make mistakes, or to use his position to help himself to money. They were desperate. Then one of them had said, "Daniel would still obey his God rather than Darius. That's how we can trap him!" So they had persuaded Darius to make a new law: "Anyone who prays to any god or to anyone except King Darius in the next thirty days will be thrown into the lions' pit." The men were sure that Daniel would not pray to Darius. He would still pray to God. They knew very well that Daniel returned to his own home three times every day. There, in an upstairs room, he would open the window's shutters so he could look towards Jerusalem. Then he would talk to God, thanking him for his care, and asking for his help in the work he did.

"It's time to go!" said one of the plotters. "He must be at home by now. They hurried out, trying to look as if they were doing nothing special. Soon, they arrived at Daniel's house. Daniel had heard of the new law, but — just as the men had expected — there he was on his knees praying to God! They had him!

They rushed to the king. Darius was dismayed. He liked and admired Daniel. He certainly did not want him to die. He just hadn't thought about him when he had agreed to the new law. But now, although he tried all day, he could find no way of saving him. "You have made the law", Daniel's enemies reminded him. "It has to be obeyed!"

"Daniel," Darius said to him sorrowfully, "I cannot save you. I pray that your God, whom you serve so faithfully, will be able to save you." Then Daniel was thrown down into the pit of lions. A great stone was rolled over the entrance, and the king went back to his palace.

All night, Darius could neither sleep nor eat. As soon as it was light, he hurried back to the lions' pit. When he got near the lions' den, he shouted, "Are you safe, Daniel? Has God saved you?"

How relieved he was when he heard Daniel's voice answering him. "I'm all right, King Darius! God knew I had done no wrong — against him or against you — and he kept the lions' mouths closed all night."

When the servants had pulled Daniel up out of the pit, Darius could see that he was completely uninjured. Darius sent messages throughout his lands describing how God had saved Daniel. "Everyone must realize that Daniel's God is the great and powerful Lord who lives for ever," he wrote.

Jeremiah in the Pit

Jeremiah 38.1–13

"Well, I thought things couldn't get any worse," thought Jeremiah, trying to wipe some of the mud off his face. "I was wrong; they have got worse." The mud made a squelching sound as he tried to move his legs. "At least there's no water in this well at the moment, but I do hope I don't sink any more deeply into the mud. How am I ever going to get out of here? The sides are much too steep and smooth to climb. I can't expect my friends to help me. They'd probably be arrested themselves if they tried."

Jeremiah didn't have many friends. He had plenty of enemies though. His special job made him very unpopular in Jerusalem. This job was to report God's messages to the people. This usually meant that Jeremiah was reminding them of how they had disobeyed God, and this was not what the people wanted to hear at all. In fact, it made the people so angry, that they tried to stop Jeremiah talking to them at all. They tried ignoring him, putting him in prison, and ordering him to stay in one house all the time. But he would not stop telling them what God wanted him to say. Only one man stood by him in all this trouble   Baruch. Baruch was always willing to help in any way he could. When Jeremiah couldn't leave the house, he used to write down Jeremiah's messages from God and take them to the king. Once, he even had to go into hiding with Jeremiah. Now, these enemies were trying to get rid of Jeremiah once and for all. "He'll either drown if it rains or starve to death down that well," they said to each other, for they were sure that no one would dare to rescue him.

But one man — Ebed–Melech — *did* dare to do something. He wanted to save him. He told the king what had happened. "These men are wrong," he said bravely. "You must save Jeremiah." The king agreed, and ordered Ebed–Melech to rescue him.

Ebed–Melech collected some rope and some old clothes, and, with his friends, rushed off to the well. He shouted down to Jeremiah, "Put the rope round you, under your arms. Use the rags to pad the rope, so that it doesn't cut into you when we pull."

Jeremiah could hardly believe that anyone had been brave enough to help him. Ebed–Melech was only a servant, but he had risked the king's anger. Jeremiah knew that with friends like Ebed–Melech and Baruch he could carry on doing his difficult and dangerous job.

RESOURCE BANK 3: STANDING UP FOR WHAT YOU BELIEVE

Stephen Dies

Acts 6.1–8.1

Stephen worked very hard in Jerusalem after he and seven others were given the special job of organizing the distribution of food. As well as doing this job very well, he spent a lot of time teaching the people about Jesus, and often God enabled him to do wonderful things, such as healing those who were sick.

Some people, however, disliked Stephen telling others about Jesus. They were jealous, too, of his popularity and his power. Unable to defeat Stephen in argument, these enemies persuaded some men to tell lies about him. "Spread this story around," they said. "Say that Stephen has told lies about Moses, and even about God!"

The religious leaders believed these lies about Stephen. They had him arrested and put him on trial. The false witnesses came and told their story. Then Stephen was given a chance to defend himself. He knew that he was in great danger, but he spoke out bravely about his beliefs. What he said caused great anger. The members of the council were furious. But Stephen angered them even more. He told them that God was showing him a glimpse of heaven, and that he could see Jesus there, in the honoured place next to God. When Stephen told his enemies this, they immediately dragged him out to kill him.

As he was dying, Stephen prayed to God. "Forgive them for doing this," he said. "Don't remember this against them." And then he died.

One of the men who was watching, agreeing with what was happening, was Saul.

Paul Stands Firm

2 Corinthians 11.16–33

Paul made many enemies while he travelled around telling people about Jesus. Often, these enemies were very powerful, and they tried their best to stop him speaking out. In one of his letters to the people living in Corinth, he writes about the problems all of this caused.

"While my friends and I were in Asia, we were often in terrible trouble. Our enemies were determined to stop us by ill–treating us. At times, things were so bad that we really thought we might be killed. But all of this just led us to trust in God the more.

"People have often upset us greatly by the cruel and unfair things they have said. They have even called us fakes, when we have only been trying to help them. At times we have had to work very hard, just to get enough food to stay alive. Even then, we have often been hungry. We have been in great danger on the sea. Three times the ships I travelled in were wrecked in violent storms. Once I spent a day and a night in the sea waiting to be rescued. Often I have gone without food, water and sleep. Five times I was given the thirty–nine lashes by the Jews. Three times I was whipped by the Romans. I have been thrown into prison many times, and once I was stoned. We have been in many other difficult and dangerous situations — such as riots — in which our lives were threatened.

"But even though we have been in a terrible condition — beaten, almost dying, grief–stricken, and very poor — really we have had the most important things — the love of God, and the satisfaction of knowing that we are serving him. Knowing that God loves us and that we are serving him, is far more important to us than all these troubles."

RESOURCE BANK 3: STANDING UP FOR WHAT YOU BELIEVE

Armour for the Battle

Ephesians 6.10–20

At the end of his letter to the believers in Ephesus, Paul wrote about the battle in which he and they were fighting. This is the battle between good and evil. Paul described a "picture" of a soldier putting on his armour and his weapons, ready for a battle. (His readers would have been able to imagine easily a Roman soldier dressed like this, as they saw many such soldiers in their town.) Paul is using this as a picture of a Christian, and the various pieces of armour and the weapons are the various gifts God has given his followers, with which they can protect themselves and resist the enemy. Here is what Paul writes:

"So, remember that God is very powerful and you yourselves can use his power when you obey him. Make use of everything he has given you for your protection. That way, you will not give up when difficulties trouble you.

"So, buckle on the belt of truth round your waist. Wear the breastplate of righteousness. Your feet should be shod with the Good News about Christ, which brings peace to people. Then, to give you even more protection, pick up the shield of faith, to defend yourself against the enemy's attacks. Wear the helmet of salvation. Last of all, take your sword of the Spirit, the Word of God. And remember to pray — for yourself and for others — all the time."

In the Pit

Read the story called "Jeremiah in the Pit" on page 108.

Jeremiah was in the pit. He was thrown into the bottom of a deep dark well. At the bottom all was mud and slime.

Activity

- Imagine you are Jeremiah. Describe what it felt like to be in the mud at the bottom of the well. Remember he would have been able to see very little.

- Draw a circle the size of a dinner plate on a piece of sugar paper.

- Cut out your circle.

- Draw a smaller circle, the size of a saucer, in the middle.

- Imagine you are Jeremiah at the bottom of the pit. You look up and all you can see is the circle of sky through the top of the well. Draw what Jeremiah could see inside the smaller circle using pastels.

- The small amount of light let in at the top of the well would have allowed Jeremiah to see a little of the inside of the well. Draw the inside of the well inside the larger circle using pastels.

Roman Soldiers

Read the passage called "Armour for the Battle" on page 111.

Activity

- Investigate the armour worn by a Roman soldier in the first century AD.

- Draw each piece of armour, and next to it write the Christian "armour" that matches it.

- Under each piece of armour, write why you think Paul chose that piece of armour for that particular word.

  Example:

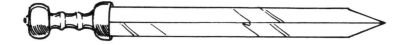

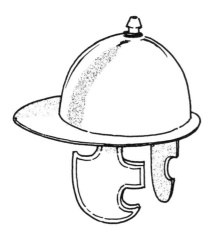

The Daniel Jazz

Read the story of "Daniel and the Lions" on page 107.

The story of Daniel has been set to music as *The Daniel Jazz* by H Chappell (Novello). *The Daniel Jazz* emphasizes that Daniel stood up for his beliefs: he kept praying even when he knew it could get him into trouble. Here is part of *The Daniel Jazz.*

Darius the Mede was a king and a wonder.
His eye was proud, and his voice was thunder.
He kept bad lions in a monstrous den.
He fed up the lions on Christian men.

Daniel was the chief hired man in the land.
He stirred up the jazz in the palace–band.
He white–washed the cellar. He shovelled in the coal.
And Daniel kept a–pray–in': "Lord, save my soul."
Daniel kept a–pray–in': "Lord, save my soul."
Daniel kept a–pray–in': "Lord, save my soul."
Daniel kept a–pray–in', Daniel kept a–prayin': "Lord, save my soul."

Activity

- Read this part of *The Daniel Jazz* through until you are familiar with it.

- Try tapping a "one, two" beat on a drum or tambour. The first tap should be harder than the second: ONE two, ONE two, ONE two. When you can hold the rhythm, try speaking the first verse to a "one two" rhythm.

- Now tap in a "one, two, three, four" beat. Make the first tap harder than the rest: ONE two three four, ONE two three four, ONE two three four. Try speaking the second verse to this rhythm.

- You might like to present your part of *The Daniel Jazz* alongside the story of "Daniel and the Lions" in an assembly.

Standing Up for your Beliefs

Read the stories of Stephen and Paul on pages 109 and 110.

Both Paul and Stephen suffered for their beliefs. Christians try to remember people who have stood firm for their faith. On certain days they remember particular saints: Stephen is remembered on 26 December. Paul is remembered on 29 June.

 Group activity

- Try to find out about ten other people who stood up for their faith. Select one for each month of the year.

- How could you make a calendar for a Christian to remind them of a different person who stood firm for their beliefs each month? The calendar needs only to have the months on, not the days.

Think about it

Many of the people who are remembered for standing up for their faith are called saints. For every saint who is remembered there are thousands of ordinary Christians who have stood up for their faith who are forgotten.